BASTARD
CHOOSE MY IDENTITY

BASTARD
CHOOSE MY IDENTITY

CHRISTIAN ERNST
LARS HARMSEN
ANDRÉ RÖSLER
ULRICH WEISS

This book is dedicated to everyone we met on our travels,
but also to everyone who stayed at home

7   **Ruediger John** . . . . INTRODUCTION

DESIGN / ILLUSTRATION / PHOTOGRAPHY

13   **IDENTITY**
68   **EVERY DAY**
108   **RIDE**
160   **PLAY**
204   **BRANDING**
252   **HOME**
286   **RELIGION**
336   **TALK**

PROSE / POEMS

59   **Selim Özdogan** . . . . LOST WITHOUT STORIES
         OHNE GESCHICHTEN AUFGESCHMISSEN
99   **László Csiba** . . . . POEMS
         GEDICHTE
139   **Sudabeh Mohafez** . . . . STONE QUARRY
         STEINBRUCH
195   **Ilija Marinow Trojanow** . . CLONING GODS, READING BAR CODES
         POEMS
243   **José F. A. Oliver** . . . . HE-MOON AND SHE-MOON
         GEDICHTE
279   **László Csiba** . . . . PENCIL AND PAPER
         BLEISTIFT UND PAPIER
325   **Radek Knapp** . . . . THE LOVE OF SLOWNESS
         DIE LIEBE ZUR LANGSAMKEIT

INDEX

373   **FONTS**
387   **INTERVIEW / AUTHORS / CREDITS**

HUMAN BEING – PERSON – COMMUNITY – INDIVIDUAL – CULTURE – COMMUNICATION – COGNITION – IDENTITY – AUTHENTICITY

RUEDIGER JOHN

A human being is a living creature. Person (*Lat. persona:* **face, actor's mask**) represents images of roles in ceremonial rites. A human being is a person as a personage with an accumulation of masks. Community is formed when there is a continuing agreement on rituals (*Lat. ritus:* **a uniformed form or manner governing actions**). Community is the responsible integration of individuals (*Lat. individuus:* **indivisible**), with a focus on shared values (*Lat. valere:* **estimate, judge**). Culture means participation in a community. Human beings create and are a part of their culture (*Lat culturare:* **to foster, care**). Culture makes a human a person. Culture is a reflective process (*Lat. reflectere:* **to bend, correlate back**; *Lat. procedere:* **to go forward**) specific to every community ensuing traditions (*Lat. tradere:* **deliver, betray**) and serving to differentiate (*Lat. dif-:* **set apart**; *ferre:* **to carry**) its society and social (*Lat. socius:* **companion**) subsystems (*Lat sub:* **under, below**; *Gk. syn-:* **together**; *histanai:* **to place, cause to stand**). The processes of social reflection are processes of communication (*Lat. communicare:* **to share**). Communication is a coherent (*Lat. cohaerere:* **to relate, adhere**) multilogue (*Gk. multi:* **many**; *logos:* **studies, discourse, opinion**). Contact (*Lat. con-:* **together**; *tangere:* **to touch**) is a social prerequisite for communication, and perception (*Gk. aisthesis:* **conscious sensory experience**) is an individual prerequisite for contact. Perception is a subjective (*Lat. subjectus:* **to subdue, to be under authority**) action. Action is the result of the individual process of cognition through primary experience (*Lat. primus:* **basic, primary, direct**; *Lat. experiri:* **to try**). Education is the guided individual process of gaining knowledge. Communication of the processes of cognition is participation in the processes of social reflection. Education and primary experience are cultural processes which form identity. Identity (*Lat. identitas:* **sameness**) is the ability to reconciliate the individual and the person. Consistency (*Lat. consistere:* **to unite, stand firm**) is authenticity (*Gk. authentikos:* **original, as a matter of principle**). Authenticity is an ideal (*Lat. idein:* **to see**). Ideals are abstractions (*Lat. abstrahere:* **to drag away, to deduce**) as cultural absolutes and are (collectively accepted and derealized) constructs of reality providing a society with meaningful common dreams and visions (objectives and wishful thinking).

GLOBALIZED CULTURE, CONSUMPTION AND IDENTITY

RUEDIGER JOHN

„Culture is a collective process of ascribing values generated by cognition. When we behold a thing or idea, we do nothing less than construct an image of it in our minds that is in tune with our way of seeing things. The supposed appreciation of the world around us is always simultaneously a display of our ignorance." (D. Granosalis)

Searching for identity through consumption

The modern search for identity is based to a great extent on the acquisition of cultural codes. Due to a surge in the global supply of symbols that serve as substituting signifiers and are reinforced by the constant stimulation of our affects through the media, the consumer creates for him or herself a patchwork identity, made up of fragments stemming from a host of differing cultures. And yet decorating the self with code elements does not mean that culture-specific societal references have been internalized to the point of us feeling a commitment to a given culture. One example is the recent trend in our latitudes of marking the body with so-called "tribal tattoos". Such a tattoo does not bring us any closer to the Maori culture, or any other culture, for that matter. Instead, such a tattoo expresses our desire of returning to the archaic and the unconditional.

One does not simply become an integral part of a given culture, but rather trends and fads decide on the validity of a person and give proof that one is capable of becoming integrated as an individual. At first glance, this seems to be the more agreeable option. Who wants to cling, or even feel dependent on one thing or idea in our fast-paced, resilient world: even if we truly are dependent. In fact, we are recipients, members of consumer target groups, who perform quasi-religious acts of substitution in the name of cultural self-conception.

At the same time, the very act of searching for identity has turned into one of pseudo-individualizing in the desperate attempt of being special and unique. And this, in spite of the fact that all participants in the markets have the exact same palette of products and symbols to choose from. This is where dynamism and resilience come into play, serving as important differentiating and eligibility markers. Forecasting trends, or even setting them, or discovering something exotic is more important than recognizing their levels of meaning and significance within a given social context. Affluent societies produce pseudo-hybrids: style nomads. Also the so-called counter-culture (especially popular culture) which serves us with its many antitheses and is marked by non-conformist behavior, functions as an engine with a mediating nature in regard to identity formation within the economic realm. And it is through this phenomenon that the consumer has internalized a crucial part of the neoliberal value framework, as well as simultaneously seriously maimed the late 18th century revolutionary cry for personal freedom.

Postindustrial societies are characterized by their mode of production: it has gone from one based on need to an economy based on want. That is to say that their economies are no longer optimized to fulfill existential needs, but rather to efficiently detect, produce and satisfy consumer wants, since the basic needs of their citizens have already been met. Having taken this approach, economic strategies have gained a special influence on cultural change, role playing patterns and rituals, as well as on how meaning and significance are ascribed. The fetish nature of brands and logos is a telling example of this.

Internationalization

At the same time, economic internationalization exports these standards, which are equal to that of a cultural imperialism, especially to nations and cultures that have already been hurt by colonialism. This often causes even greater dependence, since it, on the one hand, leads to an asymmetry in the markets and, on the other hand, because rigid power relations set in: a neo-colonial process, so to speak. Big development projects, for instance, such as those coordinated by the World Bank are often nothing more but a diversion of the subsidies granted to receiving countries to the benefit of the economies of the giving countries. They fail to take the specific dynamics of the countries on the receiving end into account, or assess the kind of impact they have on them. Really sustaining developmental aid to support the domestic economic development, such as granting micro-loans, is rare: this kind of aid would actually help lead the receiving countries to independence.

Free Trade

The doctrine which asserts that free trade ultimately will lead to wealth from which everyone will benefit, fails to contend that only a cohesive, secure and legal framework – which is based on social development – is capable, under the control of law, of equalizing power relations. Furthermore, emerging markets and economically weak nations have never been able to develop by immediately switching to a free market. It is ensued only through balanced protectionist policies and through the strengthening of their domestic markets. The United States and China have done this, and continue to do so. As have Ireland, in Europe, and up into the 1980s, this was to a great extent the case in Japan.

Economized Globalization

Globalized competition is not open and not equal. The national trade barriers set by powerful nations deny emerging nations market access, especially those countries whose chief commodities are agricultural or raw-materials. The sweatshop conditions that can be seen in the textile industry in Bangladesh, for example, are a result of one-sided developmental aid to this industry, coupled with cost-efficient-oriented outsourcing projects initialized by Western corporations. And in China, the devastating effects on the environment, and the lacking labor protection laws persist because the commodities produced there for export are not subject to the same environmental and ethical codes which are enforced in central Europe. The early capitalistic feudal structures that can be seen in India are supported by two fatal supplements: the caste system and an elite that has been educated internationally.

Since legal order within societies is defined on a state level, multinational corporations use their mobility to evade balancing legal and ethical responsibilities. In addition, international trade transactions are not regulated in a way so that many or even everyone can participate equally, but rather are governed by processes of monopoly formation, a phenomenon which Adam Smith and John Maynard Keynes, often misappropriated as leaders of neoliberal aims, have called great dangers and "an evil". Companies and persons that are mobile and less anchored to a nation state make greater (short-term) profits than those with fixed locations of business. Under such circumstances, capital has the greatest degree of mobility and its flow requires the least amount of self-liability in regard to ensuring economic and ecologic sustainability and social responsibility. This is also due to the fact that capital is perceived as dematerialized property and productive force sui generis. Shareholders do not feel like property owners with obligations, but like capital lenders in a permanent state of transit.

Globalization and Community

The process of globalization does not induce development and security of personal freedom and safety, nor does not define its value system nationally, yet still remain binding. It also does not promote the sanctioning power of international law to govern human behavior. On the contrary, those developments which are shaped by culture and need to be addressed politically lag behind those of an economical and technological nature.

The lack of decisive collaboration within large political cultural areas and nation-states in regard to their obligation to represent the interests within a given community blocks the pursuit of beneficial outcomes along three dimensions: economic, social and environmental parameters (triple bottom line), and hinders the creation of a foundation upon which sustainable and resource-conscious assessments can be made. The involvement of political and economic decision-making structures supports the short-term-oriented and one-sidedness of growth paradigms, since it takes a reductionistic view of economic actions.

At the same time, consumer behavior focused on the particular interests of each individual, following the ideology that everyone has the right to own without being required to integrate, hinders that value-based conduct can become a principle within a cultural context. Commercial interests emphasize that each and every consumer is particular and autonomous, but at the same time suggests just how powerless the individual is and how limited his or her freedom of choice is: despite the fact that humanity once set out to achieve freedom. More often than not, this type of dependence is not perceived as such, since people are conditioned to be content with conforming to cultural codes as a means of expressing their socially compatible roles.

When, for instance, an investment banker participating in the World Economic Forum announces, "If you have four good friends and like what you do, it doesn't matter where you live", he expresses, first and foremost, just how limited his neoliberal understanding of community and culture really is, although his own identity has been shaped by an intact community with collective memory and traditions, such as a legal and educational system, from which he has benefited. If everyone were to draw solely on his or her circle of friends and never develop a feeling of responsibility for his or her social environment, content with merely personal business successes, there would be no modern, innovative, society balancing the individual risks and a division of labor serving as a cultural community: at best, clan-like structures with ever-changing loyalties would evolve.

Cultural crisis

Globalization is not the problem as such, in the same way that capitalistic patterns of practice are not either. The real problem is that cultures lack the strength to cultivate and enforce values outside of economic norms and widen their transnational scope successfully. Globalization enhances a cultural crisis. "Culture" is not referred to here as a mere cultural branch, which offers an array of entertainment from pure spectacle to modern free time pleasures. Simply put, culture is a society-dependent, tradition-based, cognitive and value-building ritual and reflection canon. It creates a commitment (in attitude and behavior) to values as conditio sine qua non in regards to ethics and morals, and laws and regulations ensue. In individuals, it also creates the cognitive ability in dealing with complexity, which is essential to the existential and personal search for identity and freedom: both are crucial requirements for democracy.

BASTARD

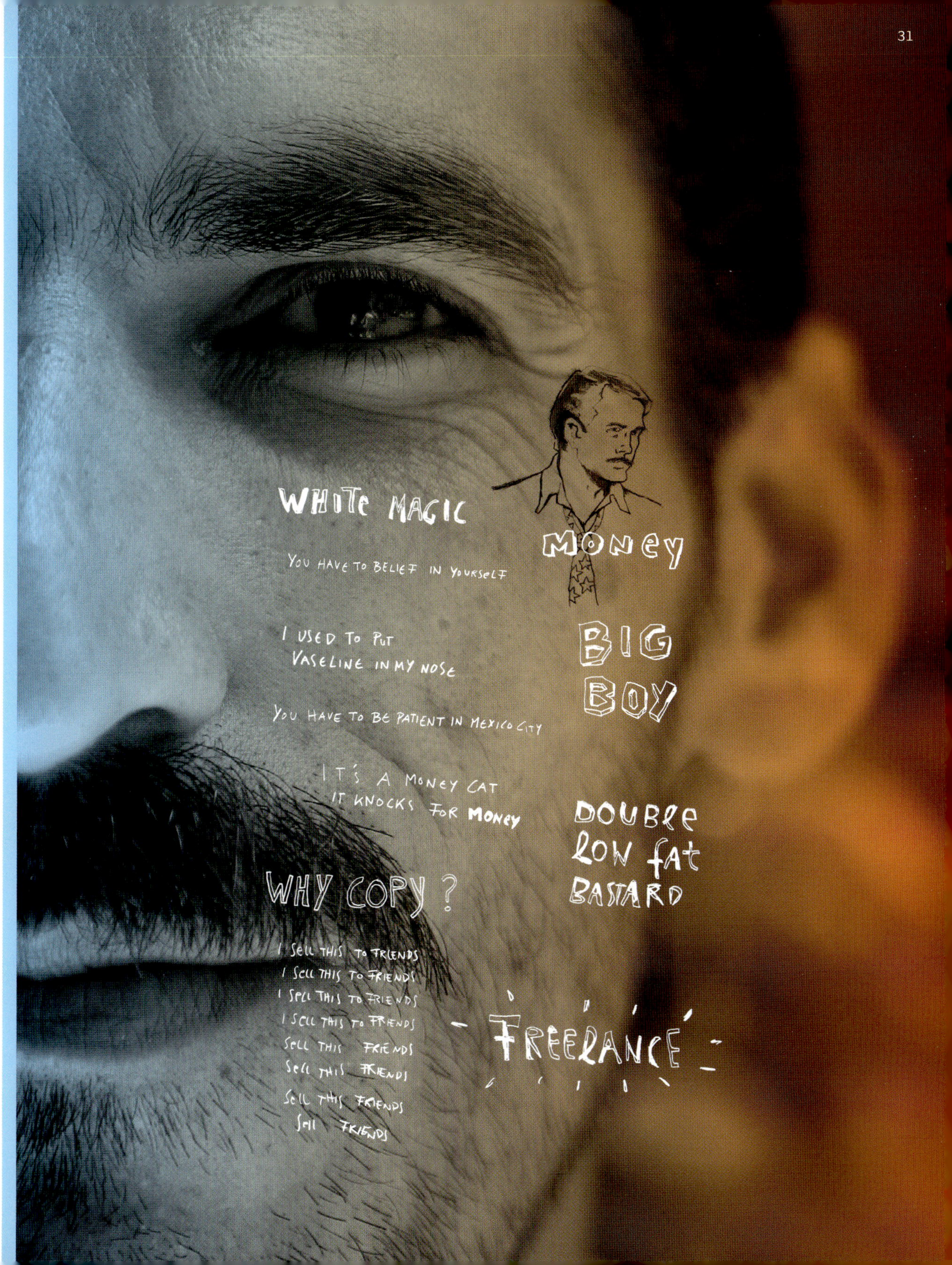

WHITE MAGIC

YOU HAVE TO BELIEF IN YOURSELF

I USED TO PUT
VASELINE IN MY NOSE

YOU HAVE TO BE PATIENT IN MEXICO CITY

IT'S A MONEY CAT
IT KNOCKS FOR MONEY

WHY COPY ?

I SELL THIS TO FRIENDS
I SELL THIS TO FRIENDS
I SELL THIS TO FRIENDS
I SELL THIS TO FRIENDS
SELL THIS FRIENDS
SELL THIS FRIENDS
SELL THIS FRIENDS
SELL FRIENDS

MONEY

BIG
BOY

DOUBLE
LOW FAT
BASTARD

- FREELANCE -

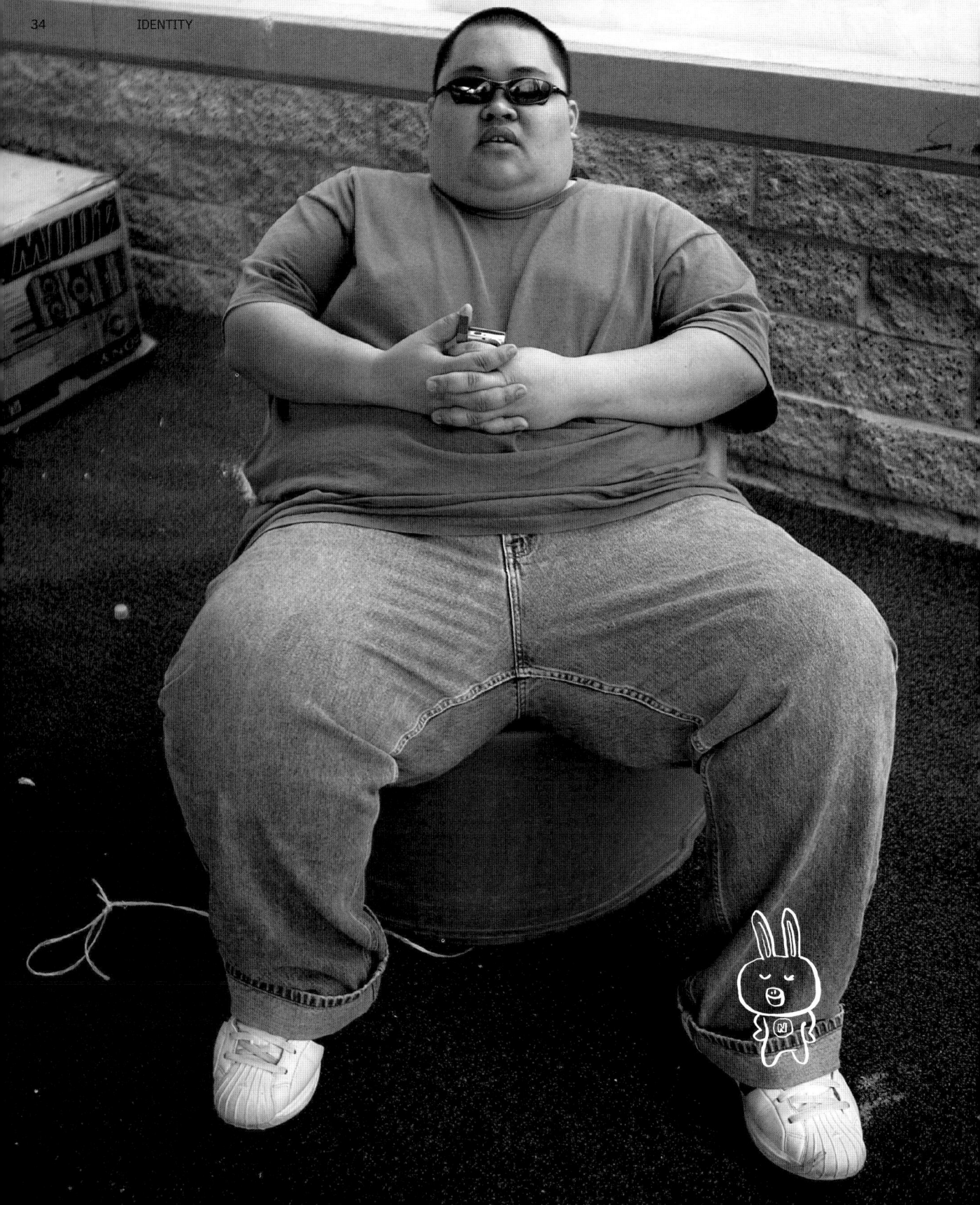

GENDER DRUG MAGIC
GENDER DRUG MAGIC
GENDER DRUG MAGIC
GENDER DRUG MAGIC
GENDER DRUG MAGIC
GENDER DRUG MAGIC

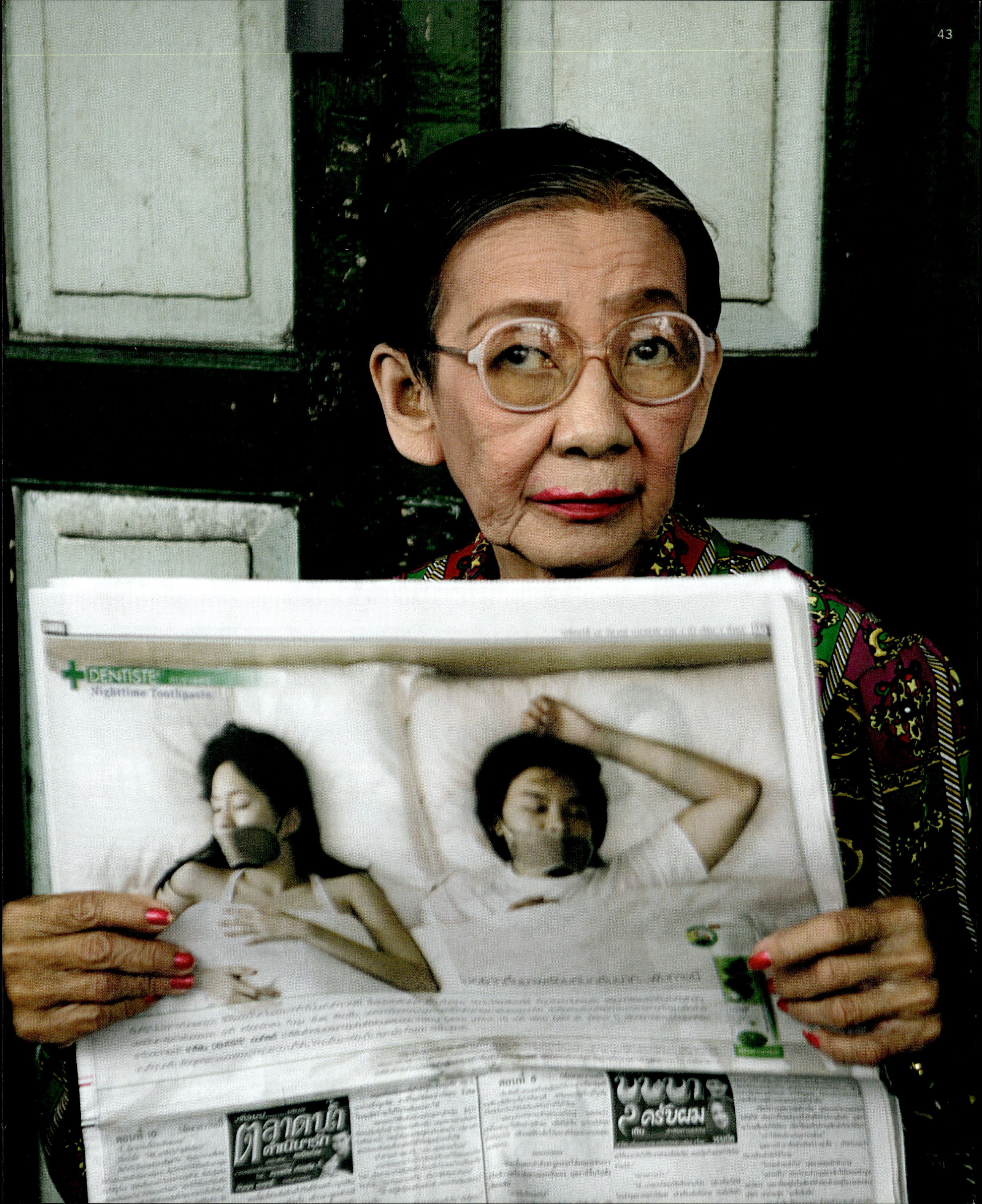
DENTISTE
Nighttime Toothpaste

LOST
WITHOUT STORIES

OHNE GESCHICHTEN
AUFGESCHMISSEN

SELIM ÖZDOGAN

Three years old. The spinning top I'm playing with is made of tin. It is colorful, larger than both my hands together. When my mother wants to cook without being disturbed, she takes it out and I sit in the living room on the carpet with the top on a plastic mat and for hours there is no other sound than the one made by the toy. I am happy.

Seven years old. A boy in my class named Martin has a learning disability and my teacher tells me that he and I should meet once a week in the afternoon and do our homework together. We sit in Martin's living room, sinking into the couch at the coffee table, leaning forward so that we can reach the table to write. The smell at Martin's house is different than at my own, and in my memory everything there is green or maybe brown, the carpet, the sofa, the wallpaper, the curtains, the television set, the cola which Martin's mother brings us. Her hair is blond, but looks sort of dirty. A year later, when Martin doesn't come to school one day, everyone says he has got alcohol poisoning. I cannot quite understand why Martin would drink poisoned alcohol and so I'm convinced that he's completely innocent. In my mind, alcohol poisoning is like a snakebite.

Ten years. When I pass by a McDonald's where a child is celebrating a birthday my eyes become as large as saucers. But not because of the hamburgers, which I don't like. For me, a children's party at McDonald's is the purest form of adventure. Maybe it's because my mother says there is no way I will ever have one there. But beating on a pot is just not enough for me.

Like most every year, we spend our holidays in Turkey. On the first day we eat zucchini because my father likes it so much, and on the second day we get noodles with yogurt sauce because that's my favorite dish. The other children in my class prefer *Miracoli*. They don't know what they're missing.

One day I open the bathroom door and my aunt turns to face me. Wearing only a tank top, she lets out a shriek as soon as she sees me. I am taken aback by the thick black tuft beneath her ribbed shirt and run away. Later, I regret not having taken a better look.

Twelve years. Anja, Marion, Marc and I often meet to ride our bicycles through the forest together. Usually, I don't just ride, I fly through the forest, and it feels so good to be riding with my friends, where adventure lurks behind every corner. When I'm not in the forest, I'm reading *The Three Investigators or The Famous Five*. I daydream of us secretly observing criminals in action, taking on gangs, of finding buried treasure. If I had it my way, I would ride through the forest every day to better our chances. Anja figures out my innermost desire for this and tells me point blank that I'm just looking for adventure. I feel discovered and deny it.

One day when Marc and I are alone in the forest together, we see a flasher. We run for our lives. I'm scared. Adventures are supposed to feel different, aren't they? I've never really been a part of one yet.

Fourteen years. I've started reading Leonard Cohen, William Burroughs, Richard Brautigan, Knut Hamsun, Yukio Mishima. I want to become a writer when I grow up; I want to have adventures and write about them. I'm afraid of girls, they seem strange to me, even Anja and Marion. Only when I'm together with my cousin Kiymet in Turkey, who is the same age as I am, do I feel sure of myself. I hug Kiymet and try to touch her budding breasts without her noticing. We hold hands, and rest our heads on each other's laps when we watch television together. I scribble page after page in my notebook, but can't seem to find the right words to describe the way my cousin's skin feels to the touch.

Fifteen. I've started drinking alcohol, and when I've had my fill, even making it to the toilet is an adventure. Afterward, I can never remember why.

I spend my afternoons alone at home dreaming about falling in love. Or, at least, that someone will fall in love with me.

I want to be a savior. Easter holiday, Whitsun holiday, summer holiday, Christmas holiday, I always dream that on the first day back to school after the holidays, there will be a new girl in my class. A girl who has switched schools because she has lost the joy in her life. I will understand exactly how she feels; I will be able to touch her soul and save her. Through her, I will be able to save myself.

Sixteen. German social workers come to youth clubs to talk to the boys and girls with backgrounds of emigration. They tell them that they feel torn between two cultures. Every day. And after a year or so the boys and girls believe it.

I feel torn and confused because my dreams don't come true. And yet at the same time, my dreams are what is holding me together. I wouldn't mind being someone else. I wouldn't mind looking better, being cool, being able to make people laugh. I wouldn't mind being more muscular, and having the most outrageous hairdo in the entire class. But, instead, I'm skinny, shy and often get teased and picked on because of my unusually large nose. I feel ugly and often look at the ground. My body moves awkwardly. I often trip and knock things over, though I try my best not too draw too much attention to myself. The boys I call my friends are extremely cruel to me. Whenever I get the chance, I'm cruel right back. We pretend that we're only joking around. At McDonald's, we throw around sliced pickles and laugh at the children who celebrate their birthdays there. When will I finally have sex for the first time.

Nineteen. Sex hasn't changed who I am, although I always thought it would. I thought that after losing my virginity I would go through some kind of metamorphosis. In the morning, it takes me twenty minutes to blow-dry and get my hair into shape. If it happens to be raining outside, it ends up being all for nothing. I can't wear a hat with my kind of hairdo, and, as a matter of principle, I never use an umbrella. I wear only black and have got shoes with toe protection, as if there were a point to that. I listen to music that usually I am the only one to have heard of, and read books that are totally foreign to my peers. Everything mainstream I consider a load of crap. No one knows the kind of life I lead. I am desperate and I am in the firm belief that I will not live past my 25th birthday. The very thought of living longer exhausts me.

Twenty-two. Life is torture for me, though I don't yet know what failure is. Life is torture, even if at the same time I'm completely convinced that I could conquer the world. I am energetic and see the faults in others. They make too many compromises, let people walk all over them, and they lie at a pinch, sell their souls for a pittance and try to fit in just to keep the peace. I, however, get my way, and don't give a damn about money; I don't go out of my way unless I really want to, and I despise everyone who does anything the wrong way. My hatred is merciless. I am special. I don't belong to the masses. I know what's what. I've got everything figured out.

When I get low I get high, sings Ella Fitzgerald. I take all the drugs I can get my hands on. Why live a healthy life and turn 90. I automatically think that what I'm doing is the right thing, because I am breaking existing rules. And also because all of the writers I admire took drugs. I want to become a writer, there is no doubt about that. Death is, of course, an alternative, but another kind of life isn't.

I haven't actually been successful at anything in particular yet, but that doesn't matter. I am the loser who will show them all.

Twenty-six. I was probably in love with myself before and only acknowledged my good traits. Now that the swoon is over, I see myself for who I really am, and can't really understand how I once could have been so fascinated by myself. I make mistakes. I've sold-out. I make compromises. My hatred has started to subside, and sometimes there is enough room for some joy in my life, but this isn't actually something I want because I'm afraid it will make me weak. When I drink now, there's not a trace of adventure involved, but I've started drinking on a daily basis. I'm a writer, but all of a sudden not a loser anymore. It takes me great pains to get used to the idea that things are going good for me. Am I someone else now.

Twenty-nine. I stop drinking. I start to enjoy the little pleasures in life. All the people I used to hate with a passion, I now try to love. I'm not always all that successful. But I can recognize now that their actions weren't due to some inherent baseness on their part. Life just sometimes puts a person in some strange situations. I want to be free. Liberate myself from the bondage of money, sex, fame, dreams and desires. I also want to liberate myself from the bondage of freedom. In other words, I want Enlightenment. Like Buddha. Ramakrishna. Like Meister Eckhart. Like Mevlana. If it is in any way humanly possible, I would like to become one with Eternal Knowledge, see God and feel the bliss. I want to finally know which way is the right one. I am searching for the truth.

Thirty-one. There is no truth. And being enlightened is just another dream we humans chase after. I have decided that I want to stop writing because it has turned into a compulsion. I write in order to survive. And not before my dream of becoming a writer has become reality, do I discover that I can dream much greater dreams. One day, I'll be able to do something completely different from what I thought at age twenty-two was the only thing worth getting up for in the morning.

Thirty-four. I'm a trained yoga instructor and very proud of it. Nearly as proud as when my first book came out ten years ago. When I pick up the book today, I can hardly imagine what kind of person wrote it. It was supposedly me, but my memory has grown murky. What moved me back then. Where did the pleasures of that time go. Whatever happened to my obsession with recognition. Where did my naivety, my arrogance go. Where did this person go. Is he inside of me. If he is, then he is very well hidden. I can hardly find him. Why was I that way before. Why did I write in the way I did. Why are my mistakes in the past no longer embarrassing to me. When I see photos of myself with my new wave haircut, I think to myself: it is typical for teenagers to want to be something different than what they are. But what are they. What are they.

If you want to put together all of the different people of different ages to form a whole picture you have no choice but to say "I". You must make up stories, and the characters must develop. Rhyme and reason does not come automatically, and memory is a good liar. Without stories, there would only be moments, disconnected from each other. The story replaces the lack of rhyme and reason. Since I have become a writer, I tell everyone today that books have always fascinated me, even before I really was able to read them. Not the other way around. But if I were an actor, I'd tell everyone that I had already started playing leading roles in primary school. That's about just as much the truth as my story about my love for literature.

My friend Markus always says: everything has changed. Nothing ever stays the same. The only thing that has remained constant is the desire to fuck.

Does everything really boil down to that: sexual desire. If so, then we're all the same. But when we look at each other, we notice that we're very different. I change, I am the same, says Leonard Cohen. The capacity to experience sustaining emotion is rather rare, says W.H. Auden. Which desires remain. Which dreams have changed. Would I like myself if I were to spend an evening with the younger version of myself. Would I be bored, or fascinated.

And yet, people are still always talking about the rift between cultures. We all are so torn and deeply anxious because we suspect that identity is an illusion which we create for ourselves. An illusion that we just can't give up. And yet it's a big mistake to think that we're the same every day.

We are all capable of feeling a strong sense of inner peace. There is probably something inside of us that never changes. And to deny this would be a grave mistake also. There is something to be found at the end of all the illusions and pictures we create about ourselves. There is something that is more than Nothingness. We all suspect that this is true. And still, we want nothing more than to live out our individuality. But we cannot slip out of our own skin. Maybe we can sometimes depart from our minds, but neither the mind nor the skin lasts forever. Human beings don't equal themselves. They equal each other. If we can understand this with every nerve in our bodies, with every glimpse caught by our senses, with every stirring of our thoughts, with every reliving of a memory, are we then still human beings, or, already something entirely different. No questions asked.

Drei Jahre alt. Der Kreisel, mit dem ich spiele, ist aus Blech, bunt, größer als meine Hände. Wenn meine Mutter in Ruhe kochen will, holt sie ihn raus und ich sitze im Wohnzimmer auf dem Teppichboden, der Kreisel ist auf einer Plastikunterlage und bis auf das Geräusch des Spielzeugs hört man stundenlang nichts. Ich bin glücklich.

Sieben Jahre alt. Martin in meiner Klasse hat Schwierigkeiten beim Lernen und meine Lehrerin sagt, wir sollten uns einen Nachmittag in der Woche bei ihm treffen und gemeinsam unsere Aufgaben machen. Bei Martin sitzen wir im Wohnzimmer am Couchtisch, versinken im Sofa und müssen uns beim Schreiben weit vorbeugen. Es riecht anders als bei uns zu Hause und in meiner Erinnerung ist alles grün oder braun, der Teppich, das Sofa, die Tapeten, die Vorhänge, der Fernseher, die Cola, die Martins Mutter uns bringt. Ihre Haare sind blond, wirken aber schmutzig. Ein Jahr später heißt es, als Martin nicht in die Schule kommt, er habe eine Alkoholvergiftung. Mir ist nicht ganz klar, wie Martin vergifteten Alkohol zu sich genommen hat, in meiner Vorstellung ist er schuldlos. Alkoholvergiftung ist so etwas Ähnliches wie ein Schlangenbiß.

Zehn Jahre. Wenn wir an einem McDonalds vorbeigehen, in dem gerade ein Kindergeburtstag gefeiert wird, bekomme ich große Augen. Es ist nicht wegen der Hamburger, die ich sowieso nicht mag. Kindergeburtstag bei McDonalds ist für mich der Inbegriff von Abenteuer. Vielleicht auch deswegen, weil meine Mutter sagt, daß das nicht in Frage kommt. Topfschlagen ist mir zu langweilig.

Die Ferien verbringen wir in der Türkei, wie fast immer. Am ersten Tag gibt es Zucchini, weil mein Vater die so gerne mag und am zweiten Tag Nudeln mit Joghurtsoße, weil es mein Leibgericht ist. Die anderen Kinder in meiner Klasse mögen lieber Miracoli. Die wissen nicht, was ihnen entgeht.

Als ich die Tür zum Badezimmer öffne, dreht sich meine Tante zu mir um. Sie hat nur ein Unterhemd an und schreit als sie mich sieht. Ich erschrecke vor dem dichten schwarzen Busch unter ihrem gerippten weißen Unterhemd und renne davon. Später bereue ich es, nicht genauer hingesehen zu haben.

Zwölf Jahre. Anja, Marion, Marc und ich treffen uns häufig und fahren mit den Fahrrädern durch den Wald. Meistens fahre ich nicht, sondern fliege, so gut fühlt sich das an mit seinen Freunden durch den Wald zu fahren, wo hinter jeder Ecke ein Abenteuer lauern könnte. Wenn ich nicht im Wald bin, lese ich Drei Fragezeichen oder Fünf Freunde. Ich träume von Verbrechern, die wir heimlich beobachten, von Banden, mit denen wir uns anlegen, von vergrabenen Schätzen. Ich will am liebsten jeden Tag durch den Wald fahren, um die Chancen zu erhöhen. Anja begreift woher dieser Wunsch kommt und sagt: Du willst Abenteuer erleben. Ich fühle mich ertappt, leugne.

Als Marc und ich allein im Wald sind, sehen wir einen Exhibitionisten. Wir flüchten als sei der Teufel hinter uns her. Ich habe Angst. Abenteuer fühlen sich anders an. Oder? Ich habe noch nie eins erlebt.

Vierzehn Jahre. Nun lese ich Leonard Cohen, William Burroughs, Richard Brautigan, Knut Hamsun, Yukio Mishima. Ich will Schriftsteller werden, wenn ich groß bin, Abenteuer erleben und darüber schreiben. Vor Mädchen habe ich Angst, sie sind mir fremd, auch Anja und Marion. Nur in der Gegenwart meiner gleichaltrigen Cousine Kiymet in der Türkei werde ich nicht unsicher. Ich umarme Kiymet, versuche dabei unauffällig ihren knospenden Busen zu berühren. Wir halten uns an den Händen, legen beim Fernsehen den Kopf in den Schoß des anderen. Ich schreibe seitenweise in meine Kladde, aber ich kann nicht erklären, wie sich die Haut meiner Cousine anfühlt.

Fünfzehn. Ich trinke Alkohol und wenn ich genug getrunken habe, dann ist selbst der Gang zur Toilette ein Abenteuer. Doch hinterher kann ich mich nicht genau erinnern, warum das so war.

Meine Nachmittage verbringe ich allein zu Hause und träume mich zu verlieben. Oder daß sich zumindest jemand in mich verliebt.

Ich möchte ein Erlöser sein. Osterferien, Pfingstferien, Sommerferien, Weihnachtsferien, immer träume ich davon, daß am ersten Schultag nach den Ferien eine neue Schülerin in die Klasse kommt. Ein Mädchen, das aufgrund ihrer Lebensunlust die Schule gewechselt hat. Ich kann sie verstehen, ich weiß, wie sie sich fühlt, ich berühre ihre Seele und rette sie. Dadurch bin auch ich erlöst.

Sechzehn. Deutsche Sozialarbeiter erzählen in Jugendeinrichtungen den Jungen und Mädchen mit Migrationshintergrund, daß sie sich zwischen zwei Kulturen hin- und hergerissen fühlen. Jeden Tag. Die Jungen und Mädchen glauben das nach etwa einem Jahr.

Ich fühle mich ganz zerrissen und zerrüttet, weil meine Träume nicht in Erfüllung gehen. Doch gleichzeitig sind sie das einzige, was mich zusammenhält. Ich wäre gerne jemand anders. Ich würde gerne besser aussehen, cool sein, alle zum Lachen bringen, ich hätte gerne Muskeln und die abgefahrenste Frisur der ganzen Klasse. Aber ich bin dünn, schüchtern und werde oft wegen meiner ungewöhnlich großen Nase aufgezogen und gehänselt. Ich fühle mich häßlich und sehe oft zu Boden. Mein Körper bewegt sich nur ungelenk, ich stolpere und stoße oft Sachen um, obwohl ich versuche mich klein zu machen. Die Jungs, die ich meine Freunde nenne, sind grausam zu mir. Wenn sich eine Gelegenheit ergibt, bin ich auch grausam zu ihnen. Wir tun so, als sei das ein Spaß. Wir schmeißen bei McDonalds Gurkenscheiben durch die Gegend und lachen über die Kinder, die dort ihren Geburtstag feiern. Wann endlich werde ich das erste Mal Sex haben.

Neunzehn. Sex hat mich nicht verändert, obwohl ich immer geglaubt hatte, ich würde eine Art Metamorphose erleben, wenn ich nicht mehr Jungfrau bin. Morgens brauche ich zwanzig Minuten, um meine Haare in Form zu föhnen. Wenn es draußen regnet, ist die ganze Arbeit dahin. Eine Mütze kann ich mit der Frisur nicht tragen und Regenschirme benutze ich aus Prinzip nicht. Ich trage nur schwarz und in meinen Schuhen sind Stahlkappen, als würde das irgendeinen Sinn ergeben. Ich höre Musik, die kaum jemand kennt, ich lese Bücher, die meinen Altergenossen fremd sind. Alles, was die Norm zu sein scheint, finde ich scheiße. Kein Mensch kennt das Leben, das ich führe. Ich bin verzweifelt und weiß, daß ich nicht älter als fünfundzwanzig werde. Das ist mir viel zu anstrengend.

Zweiundzwanzig. Das Leben ist eine Qual, obwohl ich noch nicht weiß, was scheitern eigentlich bedeutet. Das Leben ist eine Qual, auch wenn ich glaube, daß ich die Welt erobern könnte. Ich habe die Energie und ich sehe die Fehler der anderen. Sie machen zu viele Kompromisse, lassen sich klein kriegen, lügen, wenn es Not tut, verkaufen ihre Seele für ein wenig Geld und passen sich an, um der Harmonie willen. Ich setze immer meinen Kopf durch, scheiß auf das Geld, gebe keinen fingerbreit nach, hasse all die, die es falsch machen, mit einem unversöhnlichen Hass. Ich bin etwas Besonderes, ich steche aus der Masse der Menschen heraus, ich weiß einfach, wo es langgeht. Ich habe es raus.

When I get low I get high singt Ella Fitzgerald. Ich nehme alle Drogen, die ich kriegen kann. Wer will schon gesund leben und neunzig Jahre alt werden. Ich glaube, daß das schon deswegen richtig ist, weil es gegen die geltenden Regeln verstößt. Und weil alle Schriftsteller, die ich bewundere, auch Drogen genommen haben. Ich werde Schriftsteller werden, ganz sicher. Der Tod ist eine Alternative. Ein anderes Leben nicht.

Noch nie habe ich mit etwas Erfolg gehabt, aber das ist egal. Ich bin der Verlierer, der es allen noch zeigen wird.

Sechsundzwanzig. Wahrscheinlich war ich früher verliebt in mich und habe mich nur von der besten Seite gezeigt. Jetzt, wo der Rausch der Verliebtheit verschwunden ist, sehe ich mich so, wie ich wirklich bin und kann die Faszination nicht verstehen, die ich auf mich ausgeübt habe. Ich mache Fehler, bin käuflich, gehe Kompromisse ein, mein Hass verschwindet und manchmal macht er einer Freude Platz, die ich nicht in meinem Leben haben möchte, weil ich glaube, daß sie mich verweichlicht. Wenn ich trinke, ist da nicht ein Hauch von Abenteuer zu spüren, aber ich trinke nun täglich. Ich bin Schriftsteller, aber auf einmal kein Verlierer mehr. Ich muß mich mühsam daran gewöhnen, daß es gut für mich läuft. Bin ich jetzt jemand anders.

Neunundzwanzig. Ich höre auf zu Trinken. Ich genieße die Freuden. Die Menschen, die ich früher leidenschaftlich gehasst habe, versuche ich nun zu lieben. Das gelingt mir oft nicht. Aber ich kann sehen, daß sie nicht aus niederen Motiven gehandelt haben. Das Leben bringt einen in seltsame Situationen. Ich will Freiheit. Freiheit vom Geld, Freiheit von Sex, von Ruhm, von den Wünschen und Sehnsüchten, ich möchte auch frei sein von der Freiheit. Mit einem Wort will ich: Erleuchtung. Wie Buddha. Wie Ramakrishna. Wie Meister Eckhart. Wie Mevlana. Wenn es menschenmöglich ist, möchte ich mit dem unendlichen Wissen verschmelzen, ich will Gott sehen und die Wonne spüren. Ich möchte endlich mal wissen, welcher Weg der richtige ist. Ich bin auf der Suche nach Wahrheit.

Einunddreißig. Es gibt keine Wahrheit. Und die Erleuchtung ist nur eine weitere Sehnsucht, der man hinterherrennt. Ich möchte wieder aufhören zu schreiben, weil es zu einem Zwang geworden ist. Ich muß schreiben, um zu überleben. Erst als mein Traum Realität geworden ist, sehe ich, daß ich noch größer träumen kann. Eines Tages kann ich etwas ganz anderes machen, als das, was mir mit zweiundzwanzig noch das Einzige schien, für das es sich lohnte aufzustehen.

Vierunddreißig. Ich bin ausgebildeter Yogalehrer und bin stolz drauf. Fast so stolz wie auf mein erstes Buch vor zehn Jahren. Wenn ich das Buch heute in die Hand nehme, kann ich mir die Person, die es geschrieben hat, kaum mehr vorstellen. Das mag ich gewesen sein, aber dunkel ist meine Erinnerung. Was hat mich damals bewegt, wo ist die Freude von damals, der Geltungsdrang, die Arroganz, die Unerfahrenheit. Wohin ist dieser Mensch verschwunden. Ist er in mir drin. Dann ist er gut verborgen. Ich kann ihn kaum mehr finden. Warum war ich so, warum habe ich so geschrieben, warum sind mir die Fehler von damals heute nicht unangenehm. Wenn ich Fotos von mir mit aufgestellten Haaren sehe, denke ich: Es ist ein typisches Merkmal von Jugend, etwas anderes sein zu wollen als man ist. Aber was ist man. Was ist man?

Wenn man diese Menschen verschiedenen Alters zu einem machen möchte, muß man Ich sagen, damit aus einzelnen Stücken ein großes Bild wird. Man muß Geschichten erfinden, wie es zu einer Entwicklung kommt. Denn rein logisch ergibt sich nichts und die Erinnerung ist eine gute Lügnerin. Ohne Geschichten gibt es nur Momente, ohne jeglichen Zusammenhang. Die Geschichte ersetzt die Logik. Weil ich Schriftsteller geworden bin, erzähle ich heute, daß mich Bücher fasziniert haben, noch bevor ich richtig lesen konnte. Nicht umgekehrt. Wäre ich Schauspieler geworden, würde ich heute erzählen, daß ich schon auf der Grundschule die Hauptrollen in den Theaterstücken hatten. Das ist genauso wahr wie meine Liebe zur Literatur.

Mein Freund Markus sagt: Alles hat sich verändert. Nichts ist beständig. Die letzten Jahre ist nichts geblieben, wie es war, außer: Ficken wollen.

Reduziert es sich darauf, auf den Trieb. Dann sind wir alle gleich. Aber wenn wir uns ansehen, sehen wir, daß wir verschieden sind. Ich wandle mich, ich bin der gleiche, sagt Leonard Cohen. Die Fähigkeit, dauerhafte Gefühle zu empfinden, ist eher selten, sagt W.H. Auden. Welche Wünsche sind geblieben, welche Sehnsüchte haben sich gewandelt, würde ich mich mögen, wenn ich mit irgendeiner jüngeren Version von mir einen Abend verbringen müsste. Würde ich mich langweilen oder fasziniert sein.

Und immer noch kommen Menschen und erzählen etwas von der Zerrissenheit zwischen den Kulturen. Alle sind wir zerrissen und zutiefst beunruhigt. Weil wir ahnen, daß Identität eine Illusion ist, die wir uns über uns selbst machen. Eine Illusion, die man nicht einfach so aufgeben kann. Doch es ist einer der größten Fehler, zu glauben, man sei jeden Tag derselbe.

Wir sind alle in der Lage tiefen inneren Frieden zu fühlen. Vermutlich ist da etwas in uns, das sich nie ändert. Das zu leugnen, wäre auch ein Fehler. Da ist etwas ganz am Ende der Illusionen und Bilder, die man sich macht. Da ist etwas, das mehr ist als Nichts. Wir ahnen das alle. Und trotzdem wollen wir um jeden Preis unsere Individualität ausleben. Dabei können wir gar nicht aus unserer Haut. Aber manchmal aus unserem Kopf. Doch weder Kopf noch Haut sind beständig. Der Mensch gleicht sich nicht. Aber er gleicht den anderen Menschen. Wenn das jemand wirklich versteht, mit jeder Faser seines Körpers, mit jedem Eindruck seiner Sinne, mit jeder Bewegung seiner Gedanken, mit jedem Auftauchen einer Erinnerung, ist er dann noch ein Mensch, oder schon etwas anderes. Keine Fragezeichen.

ES GIBT NOCH LEUTE DIE ZUR ARBEIT FAHREN DIE WELT IST EINFACH NICHT STEHEN GEBLIEBEN
SIE FAHREN UBAHN HEUTE WIE AN JEDEM TAG UND ICH FRAG MICH DAUERND NUR NOCH WAS
JEDERTAG SEIN KANN AB JETZT / DIE ROSEN

HAB ICH LIEGEN LASSEN / DA TRAUMEN WELCHE AM MORGEN UND ICH FRAG MICH IMMER WIEDER

WARUM EIGENTLICH DIE VERDAMMTE WELT NICHT
STEHEN BLEIBT / DER STRAUSS IN HOTELWASCHBECKEN-
WASSER FÜR WENN ES SOWEIT IST

1999「日本におけるフ
た「自由の女神像」が19
褒されました。
設置から109年目パリ
ブリッジを背景にお台

由の女神像

ATUE DE LA LIBERTE
（世界を照らす自由の女神）

を記念し、パリ市セーヌ川のシーニュ（白鳥）島に1889年に
月より1999年1月までの間、ここお台場海浜公園のこの台

海を渡った世界初の海外公開でした。

JETZT IST ES SO WEIT

UND ICH FRAGE MICH WIE ICH DICH ERREICHEN SOLL
WENN DIE WELT SICH IMMER WEITERDREHT /
MEINETWEGEN KÖNNEN SIE VERROTTEN VERMODERN
DIE ROSEN / DIE FRAU IN DER UBAHN VORHIN HAT MICH
ANGESEHEN ALS WÜSSTE SIE ALLES NUR ICH

WEISS GAR NICHTS MEHR / ICH FRAG MICH STANDIG
WIE JEDERTAG WERDEN SOLL AB JETZT UND OB DIR
BEWUSST WAR WIE WEIT ICH WÜRDE FLIEGEN MÜSSEN
UM DIR DIESE MODERROSEN

DOCH NICHT ÜBERREICHEN ZU KÖNNEN / ICH WERD DIE NACHT DURCH

MACHEN WIE DIE KIDS UND GUT DRAUF SEIN / DIE LÄCHELN HIER ALLE / ICH WERD AUCH LÄCHELN DIE GANZE NACHT LANG / WIRD GANZ EINFACH DAS SCHWÖRE ICH DIR / NIEMAND

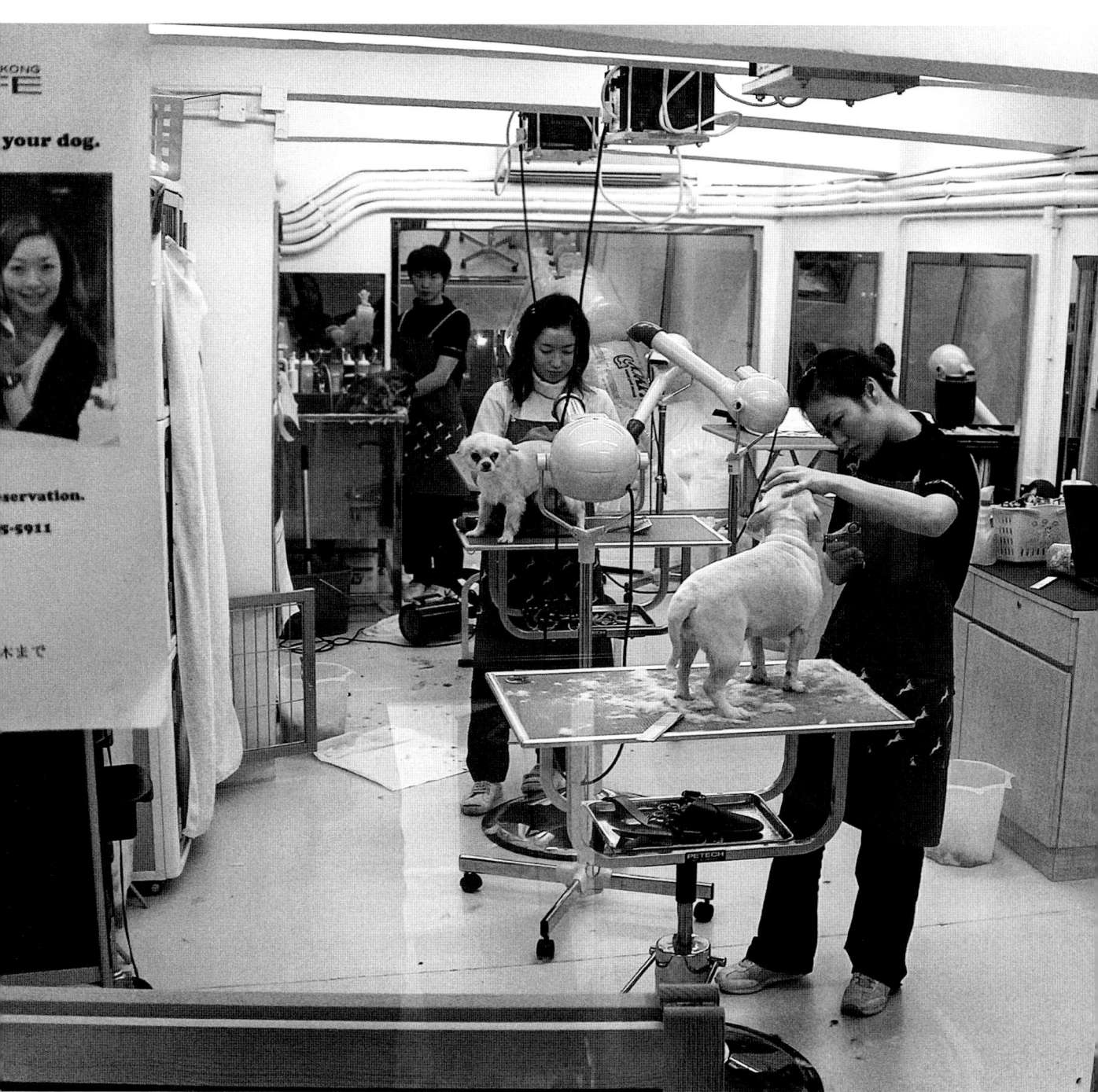

WIRD MERKEN DASS ETWAS FEHLT / ICH MACH DIE
NACHT DURCH UND VOR ALLEM ICH

WERD ÜBERHAUPT NICHT MERKEN DASS ETWAS FEHLT /
FEHLT / UND WERD AUFHÖREN MIT MEINEN SINNLOSEN
FRAGEN

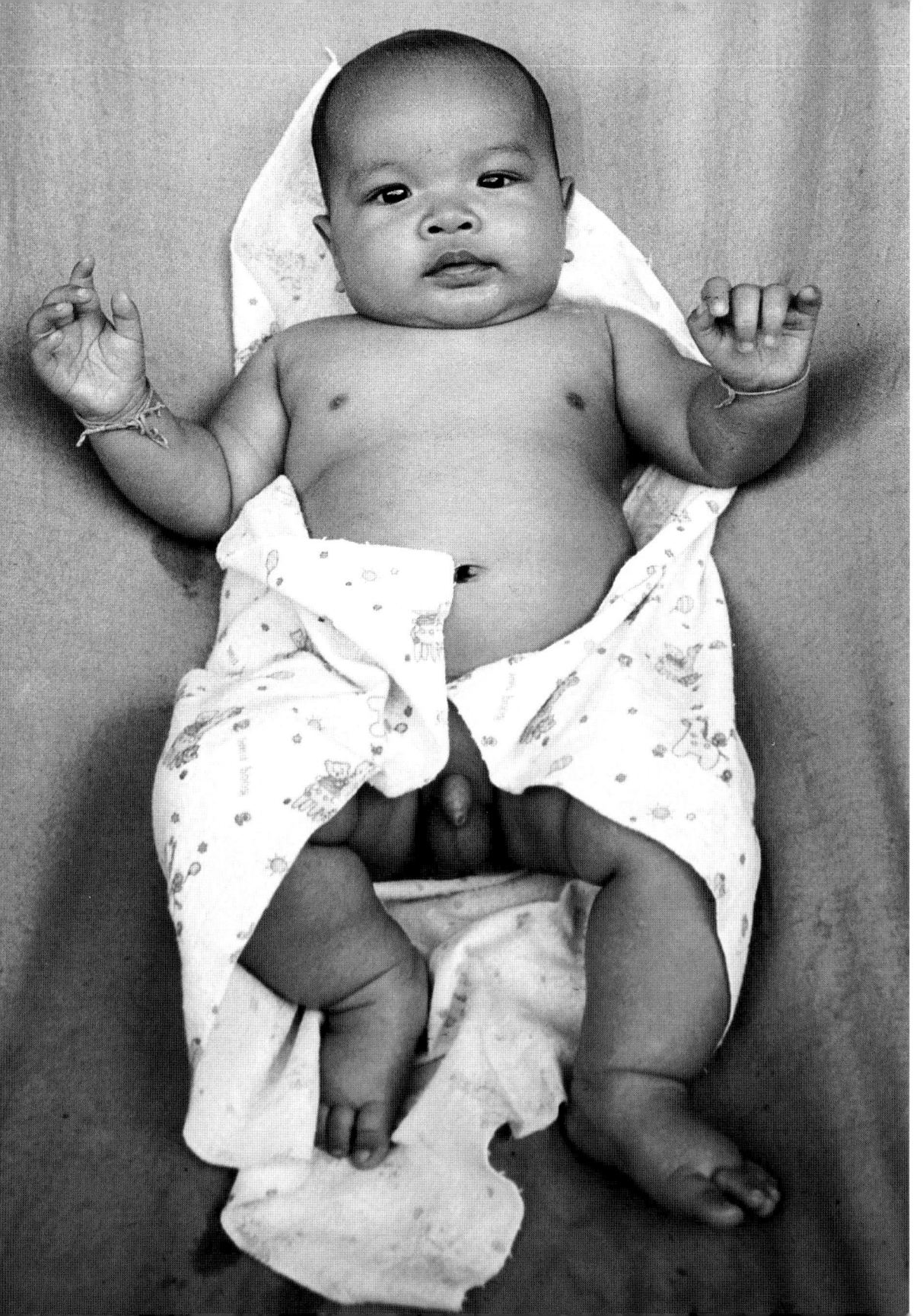

ICH KOMM NOCH AUF DEN HUND IN DIESER STADT /
KOMMT MIR VOR ALS WÄREN ES DREI ODER VIER /
STÄDTE MEINE ICH UND DIE LEUTE ALLE WIE FISCHE
IM WASSER NUR ICH DENK DAUERND AN DEN DRACHEN
DEN WIR

HABEN STEIGEN LASSEN LETZTEN HERBST UND WIE
WIR ÜBERLEGT HABEN WIE DIE WELT WOHL AUS SEINEN
AUGEN AUSSIEHT WENN ER HOCH AM HIMMEL STEHT
/ DUNKEL UND ECKIG HAST DU GESAGT UND ICH FAND
DICH UNROMANTISCH / LASS UNS WEGFLIEGEN
IRGENDWOHIN HAST DU GERUFEN / WARUM MUSSTEST
DU UNBEDINGT OHNE MICH UND

HIERHER FLIEGEN WO ALLE LAUFEN UND
LÄCHELN UND LAUFEN / FAST ALLE / NUR ICH
WEISS NICHT MEHR WIE DAS GEHT UND GLEICH
/ ICH GLAUB GLEICH / BLEIB ICH STEHEN IN
DIESEM WIRRWARR AUS SACKGASSEN UND
EINBAHNSTRASSEN

WENN SCHON DIE WELT NICHT DANN ICH / ICH STELL
MICH HIER HIN UND WERD LEERE ATMEN / DAS MIT DEN
ROSEN IST SCHADE / ICH HÄTTE SIE AUF DEN BODEN
LEGEN KÖNNEN HIER MITTENREIN IN DIE LÄRMENDE
FREMDSTADTSTILLE

DIE PFÜTZEN SIND WASSERSCHLAUCHKINDER KEIN
REGEN WEIT UND BREIT / HIER MUSS ER IRGENDWO
SEIN DIESER FRIEDHOF DEN DU DIR AUSGESUCHT HAST
UM AUFZUHÖREN / ES WIRD VON FREMDEN WIMMELN
DIE HALBE STADT WIRD DA SEIN UND ICH MITTENDRIN
UND DIE ROSEN IM HOTEL UND DU IN DER TOSENDEN
ERDE DIE

KNATTERT UND DRÖHNT UND SONNENVERBRANNT AUF
WASSER FÜR MORGEN WARTET / JEDENTAG

POEMS

GEDICHTE

LÁSZLÓ CSIBA

HUNGARIAN FOR FOREIGNERS

Language – you're hurting me.
(R.D. Brinkmann)

the mother's language
out of a thousand languages
why exactly this language?
the father's silence
out of a thousand fathers
why exactly this father?
the language of the country's
fathers
have i passed through its
gate?
the bread is fresh
i eat the bread of remembering
and am still hungry
kenyér sajt kövek
i eat the bread of forgetting
and am still hungry
i eat the bread of names
i eat the bread of voices
and am still hungry
i eat the bread of questions
and am still hungry
i eat the bread of smells
closets stairwells lavatories
and decaying fruit

i eat the bread of incandescent dust
where the light wildly reels
i listen to the insects whisper
tücskök bogarak legyek
i eat the bread of dreams
and fill my hat with fish
i eat the bread of good-byes
and there is no turning back
i eat the bread of foreignness
and the hunger does not stop
have i put down roots here
to spite the wind and tides?
lovak fecskék verebek
i break my motherword
and the mother breaks in me
i look at the origin of all beginnings
and my eyes are shattered
i constantly hear the silence pulsate
and shut my ears
of the thousand biographies
why exactly this one biography?
i strike the boulder
with my stave again and again
I WANT WATER
the song that disappeared
will be sung anew
lesson one:
(no, not that feeling)
objects are leaving this place
of events
a pohár a hegedü
virágcserepek

lesson two:
a playing die made of glass
calls me by my name
reveals who i am
    who i have been
lesson three:
letters burn
on a torn-out page
ablak ez vagy ajtó?
my tongue is dry
my lips numb
a fa zöld
a föld barna
a mothersound a fatherword
colors return from the ashes left by
the sentences
what is left
is an endless fall day in march
through which i go
in Germany

    bread cheese stones
    horses swallows sparrows
    cicadas bugs fly
    the cup the violin
    flower pots
    is that a window or
    a door?
    the tree is green
    the earth is brown

THERE IS THE BRIDGE

i try to listen to find out
if i can hear
the river,
there is the shore
there is the house
with my previous life
    the grease on my bread
    the salutations
    and how it was
and here
    the failures
    the forest paths
    the misunderstandings
    the contradictions
    the insights
    the insinuations
there the obsolete newspapers
here a fleeting elegance
    of an indiscernible present time
    through which i travel
    without valid papers
    just like that
    as a tourist would
in my understanding

FACT REMAINS

we have faced up to
life,
thought up stories,
laughed about all kinds of
nonsense,
tamed lions,
not always
mocked the
system,
fact remains:
we still have not got our opinions
straight
as always
we are
flogged by desires,
off and on
overcome by pity
but nothing is the way
it once was,
we do not fool ourselves,
we take nothing personally,
we are interested in
simple things
the shape of stones
the life of plants
the whistling of the wind
the dying of birds
for example

WHAT IS A THOUGHT AFTER ALL?

somewhere
someone is pondering
somewhere
someone is questioning
and struggling with themselves
somewhere
someone is playing music
egy utolsó
elpattant pillanat
and everything will take on
a different meaning
which is as wonderfully
simple as a
butterfly's flight

"one last,
detached moment"

TERRE DES HOMMES

i have in the living room
secretly planted three trees
have courageously entered into
the morning's vocabulary
multiplied the good moments
scraped the colors of lies
from the closet
painted over the frescoes ...

i have with a 2B pencil
discreetly completed
the month of august '54
had some green tea ...
spoken politely with Jesus
on the telephone
(nine cents a minute)
posited God
the question: will mankind be able
to save creation?
(the number you have dialed is no longer
in service)
a short-lived shaking
of my belief
in the incarnation of the word ...

have torn up the letter to Nietzsche
then glued the shreds
back together again and sent it off
(according to the digital display: 17.2
grams of words)

i have tried
to understand the intelligence of light
as well as the wisdom
of darkness,
i have speculated
on the gender of
THE LAST HUMANS
played with the idea
of a simulated resurrection ...

i have seen
a large brown hope
on the face
of a sparrow
then swept the kitchen
gone shopping
come back and
done the declension of home,
the ballpoint pen,
a suitcase
full of blank pages,
reused the green tea leaves
to brew a second pot
done the declension of bare skin
my presence (79 kg live weight)
homeland
the earth   Lago Maggiore
the earth   Lago Maggiore
the earth
the earth ...

UNGARISCH FÜR AUSLÄNDER

„Sprache du tust mir weh."
(R.D. Brinkmann)

die sprache der mutter
aus tausend sprachen
warum gerade diese sprache?
das schweigen des vaters
aus tausend vätern
warum gerade dieser vater?
die sprache des landes
der väter
bin ich durch dieses tor
gegangen?
das brot ist frisch
ich esse das brot des erinnerns
und werde nicht satt
kenyér sajt kövek
ich esse das brot des vergessens
und werde nicht satt
ich esse das brot der namen
ich esse das brot der stimmen
und werde nicht satt
ich esse das brot der fragen
und werde nicht satt
ich esse das brot der gerüche
der kleiderschränke treppenhäuser
aborte und faulender früchte

ich esse das brot
des weißglühenden staubes
worin sich wild das licht wälzt
ich höre dem geflüster der insekten zu
tücskök bogarak legyek
ich esse das brot der träume
und fülle den hut mit fischen
ich esse das brot der abschiede
und ein zurück gibt es nicht
ich esse das brot der fremde
und der hunger hört nicht auf
habe ich hier wurzeln geschlagen
gegen wind und gezeiten?
lovak fecskék verebek
ich breche das mutterwort
und die mutter bricht in mir
ich blicke in die quelle allen beginns
und meine augen sind zersplittert
ich höre unentwegt die stille pochen
und halte die ohren zu
aus tausend biographien
warum gerade diese biographie?
ich schlage vielmals
den felsen mit dem stab
ICH WILL WASSER
das verlorene lied
wird neu gesungen
lektion eins:
(nein, nicht diese empfindung)
gegenstände verlassen den ort
der ereignisse
a pohár a hegedü
virágcserepek

lektion zwei:
ein würfel aus glas
nennt mich beim namen
enthüllt wer ich bin
    wer ich gewesen bin
lektion drei:
buchstaben brennen
auf einer herausgerissenen seite
ablak ez vagy ajtó?
die zunge ist trocken
die lippen taub
a fa zöld
a föld barna
ein mutterlaut ein vaterwort
farben kehren aus der asche
der sätze wieder
was bleibt
ist ein unendlicher herbsttag
durch den ich gehe
anfang märz in Deutschland

> *Brot Käse Steine*
> *Pferde Schwalben Spatzen*
> *Grillen Käfer fliegen*
> *die Tasse die Geige*
> *Blumentöpfe*
> *ist das ein Fenster oder*
> *eine Tür?*
> *der Baum ist grün*
> *die Erde ist braun*

DORT IST DIE BRÜCKE

ich versuche zu lauschen
ob ich den fluß
hören kann,
dort das ufer
dort das haus
mit meinem früheren leben
    das fett auf dem brot
    die grüsse
    und wie es war
und hier
    die versäumnisse
    die waldwege
    die mißverständnisse
    die widerreden
    die innenansichten
    die zwischentöne
dort die verjährten zeitungen
hier die flüchtige eleganz
    einer unsichtbaren gegenwart
    durch die ich reise
    ohne gültige papiere
    nur so
    nach touristenart
wie ich es meine

TATSACHE BLEIBT

wir haben uns
dem leben gestellt,
geschichten ausgedacht,
über allen möglichen unsinn
gelacht,
löwen gebändigt,
nicht immer
gegen das system
gestichelt,
tatsache bleibt:
unsere meinungen haben wir
immer noch nicht geordnet
wir werden
nach wie vor
von sehnsüchten gepeitscht,
ab und an
von selbstmitleid erfaßt
aber es ist nicht mehr so
wie es mal war,
wir machen uns nichts vor,
nehmen nichts persönlich,
wir interessieren uns
für schlichte dinge
für die form der steine
für das leben der pflanzen
für das sausen des windes
für das sterben der vögel
beispielsweise

WAS IST SCHON EIN GEDANKE?

irgendwo
wird nachgedacht
irgendwo
wird gefragt
und mit sich gerungen
irgendwo
spielt jemand musik
egy utolsó
elpattant pillanat
und alles wird
einen anderen sinn haben
was wunderbar
einfach ist
wie der flug
eines schmetterlings

>   „ein letzter,
>   losgelöster Augenblick"

TERRE DES HOMMES

ich habe im wohnzimmer
heimlich drei bäume gepflanzt
bin beherzt in den wortschatz
des vormittags hineingegangen
die guten momente malgenommen
die farben der lüge
vom schrank gekratzt
die fresken übermalt ...

ich habe mit dem bleistift 2B
den august'54
unauffällig zu ende gezeichnet
grünen tee getrunken ...
in einem höflichen ton
mit Jesus telefoniert
(neun Cent pro Minute)
die frage: wird der mensch
die schöpfung bewahren können?
an Gott gestellt
(kein Anschluss unter dieser Nummer)
flüchtige erschütterung
meines glaubens
an die inkarnation des wortes ...

den brief an Nietzsche zerrissen
dann die schnipsel
zusammengeklebt und abgeschickt
(laut Digitalanzeige: 17,2 Gramm Worte)

ich habe versucht
die intelligenz des lichtes
zu begreifen
ebenso die weisheit
der finsternis,
ich habe gerätselt
über das geschlecht
DES LETZTEN MENSCHEN
eine fingierte auferstehung
durchgespielt ...

ich habe
eine große braune hoffnung
auf dem gesicht
eines sperlings gesehen
danach die küche gekehrt
eingekauft
zu hause angekommen
das heim dekliniert,
den kugelschreiber,
einen koffer
voll leerer blätter,
den grünen tee
noch einmal aufgegossen
die nackte haut dekliniert
meine anwesenheit (79 kg Lebendgewicht)
die heimat dekliniert
die erde Lago Maggiore
die erde Lago Maggiore
die erde
die erde ...

NOBODY GOES THERE ANYMORE.
IT'S TOO CROWDED.

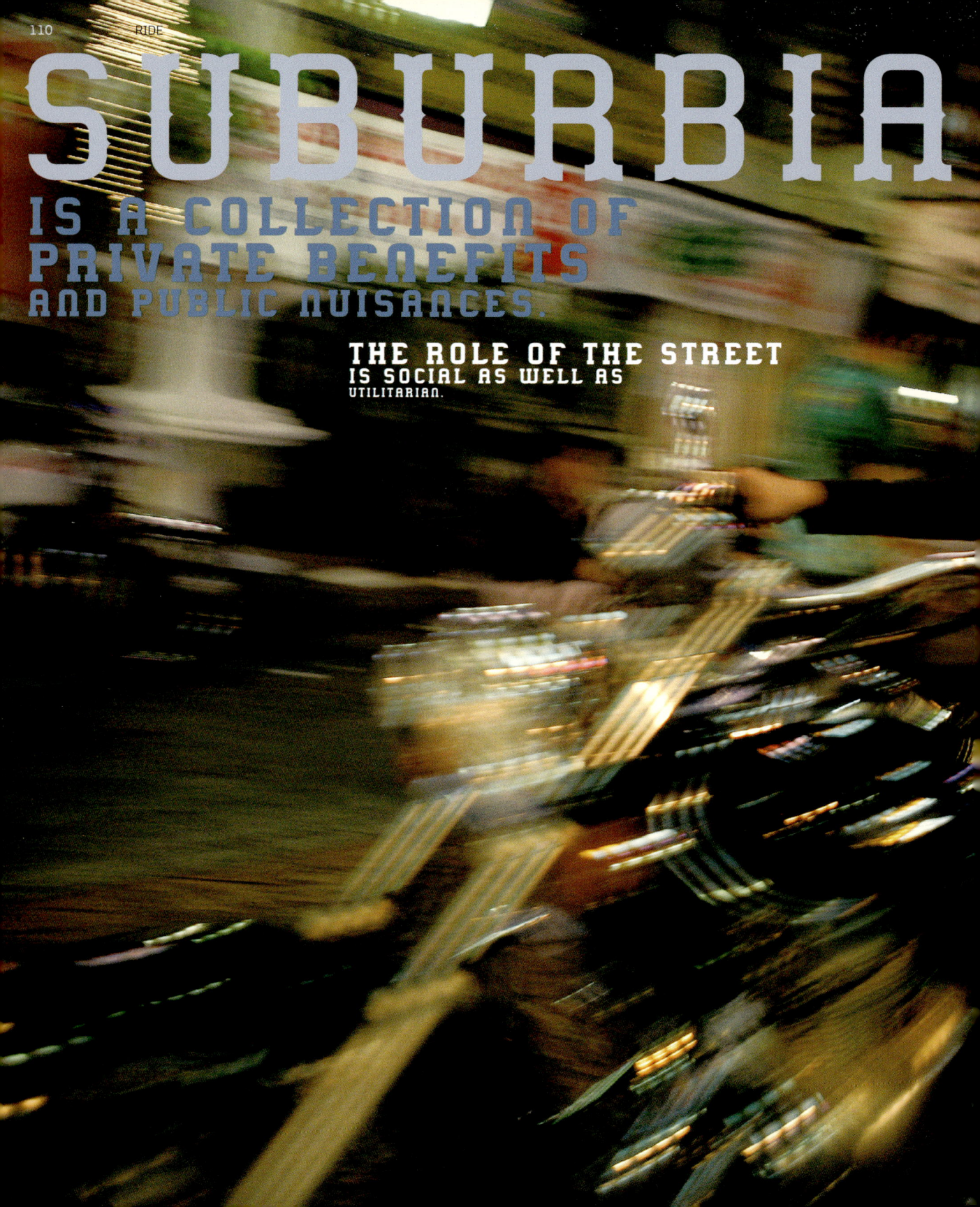

SUBURBIA

IS A COLLECTION OF PRIVATE BENEFITS AND PUBLIC NUISANCES.

THE ROLE OF THE STREET
IS SOCIAL AS WELL AS
UTILITARIAN.

"MOST OF MY TREASURED MEMORIES OF TRAVEL ARE RECOLLECTIONS OF SITTING." — —

I DO

WALK

I HATE TO WALK

IIS FUCKING BORING

IV IS MY BEST FRIEND

One town's very like another
When your head's down over your pieces, brother
(It's a drag, it's a bore, it's really such a pity)
(To be looking at the board, not looking at the city)
What d'ya mean
You seen one crowded, polluted, stinking town
(Tea, girls, warm and sweet, sweet)
(Some are set up in the Somerset Maugham suite)
Get Thai'd! You're talking to a tourist
Whose every move's among the purest
I get my kicks above the waistline, sunshine

One night in Bangkok makes a hard man humble
Not much between despair and ecstasy
One night in Bangkok and the tough guys tumble
Can't be too careful with your company
I can feel the devil walking next to me

TAKE THE BUS,
SAY HELLO TO THE DRIVER.
BOMB.
DIE.
HEAVEN.

Look at all the buses now that want exact change, exact change. I figure if I give them exact change, they should take me exactly where I want to go.

COME ALONG
AND RIDE
ON A FANTASTIC VOYAGE

SLIDE SLIPPITY SLIDE
WHEN YOU'RE LIVING IN A CITY

IT'S DO OR DIE
COME ALONG AND RIDE ON A FANTASIC VOYAGE
SLIDE SLIDE WHO-RIDE
YOU BETTER BE READY WHEN THE 5 ROLL BY
JUST ROLL ALONG- THAT'S WHAT YOU DO
JUST ROLL ALONG- THAT'S RIGHT
JUST ROLL ALONG- THAT'S WHAT YOU DO
JUST ROLL ALONG- THAT'S RIGHT
DO YOU WANT TO RIDE WITH ME, DO YOU WANT TO RIDE WITH ME
DO YOU WANT TO RIDE WITH ME, DO YOU WANT TO RIDE WITH ME
DO YOU WANT TO RIDE WITH ME, DO YOU WANT TO RIDE WITH ME
DO YOU WANT TO RIDE WITH ME, DO YOU WANT TO RIDE WITH ME

SLIDE

LET YOUR MEMORY BE YOUR TRAVEL BAG.

LING ON HER WAY

Otherwise Tokyo is great for walking.
There are no no-go areas,
and it is the best way to discover
the hidden nooks and crannies that exist
in nearly every neighbourhood.

TWO OF THE GREATEST GIFTS WE CAN GIVE OUR CHILDREN ARE ROOTS AND WINGS.

TAKE A PLANE
TO A TOWN IN MIDEAST
DRINK A COKE
AND FLY BACK

STONE QUARRY

STEINBRUCH

SUDABEH MOHAFEZ

I - Jewels beneath the skin

Every place

     inside of me is

     inexistent

          not from here

and you move your hand slowly over the goose bumps you are making on my skin, on the curve of my hip, as you say, I want to go there, with-you, I want to go, you say. Back.

Every place

     inside of me is

     inexistent

          in the outside space

          inside the world

and so I say, Why would I want to go there? What's the point of all this: going back, with-you? That is: with-me?

In a bustling airport (where else?) we argue with each other thoroughly (how else?). This place, this non-place you want to go to is missing in more than one place. For instance in this list: Mexico City, Bangkok, Tokyo, Dubai, Los Angeles. It is an example of a list where it is missing (even if this is, strictly speaking, impossible, because how can a place be missing when it does not even exist).

This place, to which we are bound and upon which we have been welded together, does not exist. This is because it is inside of me (which would suggest that it moved me, that it must have penetrated me at least at some point in time when it was given enough space to complete the change: outside-to-inside).

There are lines and patterns. There are signs, which this place has left on-and-in-me (which would suggest that this place must have existed once, or, at least, could have, because how else could it have impressed itself on me, on what I am?). This place: a jewel beneath the skin and upon the skin. Branding, piercing, signature. Signs, decipherable, indecipherable. It has left them on-and-in-me. On-and-in-you? Yes, truly. Also on-and-in-you (which is why we stop to pause for a moment, which is why at the banquet at the hotel we stop short amidst all the other guests who admire our fawn eyes and are unable to pronounce our names. The very names we both years ago separately made pronounceable. Made them pronounceable, so that we would be addressable).

But today we are (naturally) arguing thoroughly with each other in a bustling airport (where else?), and you want to go in a direction that is not inside of me. Going back, can't happen, I say.

If I do this É, you say, interrupting yourself as you move your gaze over my lips before diving down between my collar bones as we stand beside the bed still completely dressed with a rosy heat shimmering beneath our olive-colored faces. If I do this, you repeat, suddenly beginning to knead the fingers of your right hand with those of your left, tearing your gaze away from my skin and throwing it out the window behind the bushes, turning pale then, there is no going back. Fear of kissing. Fear of what might follow.

But, all the same, going back can't happen. I already mentioned that. It is with my line-drawn mouth that I say it. One temple, branded by a place that does not exist; the top of my right breast, also branded, yet still covered with lace and silk and the fine woven cotton of my shirt. I say that this place does not exist, cannot exist: this going-back-place, and I convince you of a kiss for the moment. That it is worth the risk, worth falling onto the bed for, shedding the sheddable skins, making visible the scars: marked by place we lie in distant geographies. As if it were a magnet, this non-place caused us to collide into and upon each other. This non-place out of which we are drawn. I am full of wonder as I feel the mountain in your eyes (at the hotel amidst all the other guests who admire our fawn eyes, et cetera), as I smell the desert in your voice, taste the cherry blossom in the furthest corner of your gaze and hear the dovecote's song in the air at the banquet, before I even really lay eyes upon you. Falling into each other, in succession, silently, with downcast eyes, unique, simultaneously, heads turn, no smiles: You too? How can it be? You – with your line-drawn mouth; with the branding upon your temple and at the top of your right breast where my index finger moves following the desert wind – and I. How could it come to pass?

Every place

    inside of me is

    inexistent

      in the outside space

      inside the world

and I insist that it doesn't exist: in the world it belongs to the world; to time, to corrosion, et cetera. Inside of me it is particular. I won't compare it and that is why we argue so thoroughly with each other at this ridiculous provincial airport. I will not move this place inside of me onto its copy in the outside. I want them to endure being distant and at close proximity at the same time. I want them to learn. I safeguard the (my) original. Their discrepancy does not interest me. It exists. That is sufficient. The yesterday-and-today-geographies inside of me surround me simultaneously: interpretation remains forever mystic.

There is a place you call back, on one side of it a mountain, on the other side the desert, during the day the sun shines down on it, during the night, the moon (unless there is a new moon). It is foolish to buy a ticket, to pack one's bags, make travel plans and then end up arguing with me about how I am not-coming-with-you. Foolish, considering that I have been saying No from day one.

Go with your wife. She wouldn't be going back. She would be going into the future. To a place that in her future would be original for her. Go with your wife and your child, wander through the outer shadows of the mountain. Go ahead and go. Go with wife-and-child. Go tomorrow, or go yesterday, and let your hand move over my body and not just your hand and not just over my body: be inside of me. It can happen.

We remain standing for a while (two hours after you rose up out of me, having placed this ticket between my breasts and an image of the mountain inside of me, that doesn't exist), and stand here in a bustling airport (where else?) and argue thoroughly with each other (of course). In the trembling bustle of the province surrounding you, you are unhappy (unhappy: you are going back to your wife, you will go with-her, you will devote yourself to your child, and I want for you to devote yourself to your child), I am unhappy (unhappy: hands clamped behind my burning back, standing amidst heart shards in the rain), arguing with each other about non-places (and I admit:?) It's here, I say, and you sigh. The place is here, I say, and point to the arch of one of my eyebrows. Interpretation: mystic (what else?). But how could it come to pass that I now must endure another original alongside my own? And also, and above all: How can it be that you need me to be able to keep your original?

You want your back-place to be one of ongoing encounter, continuation and reunion. I want my inside-of-me-place to be a stone quarry: a place where the earth is mightily blasted, and shapes. A quarry-place, where there is a before and an after. A stone-quarry-original: movement through my yesterday-and-today. That is what I want. It can happen.

If only we would have thought things through first, we would have saved ourselves from this figment of our imagination, this illusion of divisibility, these fantasies of the congruence of places. If we had only built upon the knowledge of life, yours, mine, then we would have shut our eyes, allowed our fingers to feel their way, mine over your body, yours over mine, then we would have silently undressed each other, aroused each other, thrust, exulted, whimpered, grunted, moaned loudly; and we would have left the places be. That would have been smart: point blank and real. It would have been an original thing to do. But, instead, we only thought about traveling and about not traveling as we celebrated our skin and our hair, as we compared the brandings upon our temples, and dipped the places into the soapy gold dust of longing. Instead of just leaving them be: the concrete, the bricks, the smog, the cars, the masses, the parks, everywhere there are these huge parks in the ravines, and then there is the thing about time: the rushing, the hurrying, the timekeeping. Some timepieces you use to clock in with, some to set an alarm, some are for measuring, for confirming; it's everywhere, this thing about time, as if it were constantly moving forward, forever straight ahead into tomorrow, and simply everything is originally copied. If we only had proceeded with more caution, we would have fallen into each other lustwardly, joywardly and we wouldn't have to go on and on about all of these places, some even divided, which apparently bind us to each other, and we wouldn't have to argue in the heart-shattered here-and-now of our fork-in-the-road to come.

In the ridiculous, bustling provincial airport that you don't-want-to-leave-without-me, your cell phone rings (of course) right in the midst of our thorough argument. It calls you to your exterior place, where I cannot be found and never will be. But it must exist, because I cannot find it inside myself, and it isn't inside of you either.

Every place

      inside of me is

      inexistent

         not from here

and your hand presses the button with the small green icon on it.

     Every place

      inside of me is

      inexistent

         in the outside space

         inside the world

and into the small silver device you say, I'll be there in two hours, and then you push the button with the small red icon on it.

II – Blind Sight

At the summit. He is lying at the top of the mountain. He can't get any higher without losing the ground beneath his feet. The climb was arduous; it took him a long time. His sun glasses, he forgot to take them with him, and now he can hardly see a thing. Snow blind. It's dangerous, he thinks to himself, but they say the symptoms disappear as soon as all the whiteness of the snow is gone, the glacier whiteness, he believes, that has surrounded him for days, ever since he reached the snowline, and didn't turn back, but continued on, continued walking. Higher, always higher, toward the top. Serpentinely, at times on the brink, traversing high plateaus, treading upon brittle blinding whiteness. A whiteness that he had to discover wasn't white at all. When he picked some up, plunged his hand into a snow-drift and held the sky crystals close to his eyes, he found blue in them. Gray, and also green. There was red, brown, and yellow, of course, and then when the color black emerged, he grew quiet deep inside. Where the static sound of thought and the rivers of the senses ring out incessantly, stillness had surged forth, and he had seated himself. In the middle of this slanted glistening desert of snow, he had seated himself, completely stunned as he started searching through scraps from physics lessons learned long ago: optics, theory of colors. But he hadn't been able to put anything meaningful together.

Later, close to the summit, the blackness had begun to dominate, it had swallowed the other colors and now only the world's darkness was left. Dangerous, he thought to himself, but they say the symptoms disappear as soon as all the whiteness is gone. He was crawling over the ice on all fours by then, over sharp corners and past even more brinks. Forget about walking upright, he thought, it isn't safe, it isn't essential. Stay close to the ground, close to the ice, to the whiteness. And then he thrust his hand out and came up empty and found, after some brief horizontal groping, the ridge to the other side:

the top. He has now reached the summit of the mountain. He can't get any higher without losing the ground beneath his feet, he thinks to himself, as he lets himself fall flat on his chest and he submerges his face into icy snow, cold, nearly frozen and still blind; he listens. Wind. Of course. And also: wind and wind. Absolutely nothing else. Silence, maybe. The silence of wind, as it were, he thinks to himself and smiles inside the snow crystals melting from his breath. He turns onto his back, props himself up partway with his elbows and his gaze searches for the city. Darkness. Gray and slippery shadows, smarting pains, in lashline his tearing eyes, in a place (somehow deep inside the eye?) that yesterday he didn't know existed. Ever since this place has started smarting and burning, and lodged a spike inside his brain, he knows of it. The retina, he thinks, as he reaches for his scarf and binds it tightly around his head, so that his eyes are covered. Whatever happens, it can't detach, he thinks to himself, it isn't under any circumstances allowed to detach. Things would never go back to normal. Not after all those days he has yet to spend on his descent. Unless he changes his mind. But then he won't need his retinas anymore. For now he opts to use his scarf, and feels the pleasant, warm pressure on his temples; the outer darkness that pushes itself in front of the brightness of the world soothes his inner pain. Latitude, he thinks to himself. One must keep one's freedom of action and make certain one has choices, he slowly completes his thought, and thinks of the serpentine descent, how it is steep, thrilling, dangerous, how his eyesight will return in the end and he sits up entirely at first. Finally, the city. That's the only reason he is here. Because of the city. Don't lose sight of your goal, he thinks to himself and breaks into a smile again. Don't ever lose sight of your goal, he thinks, and he can't keep himself from smiling at the somewhat modified repetition. He smiles until he can't help but laugh out loud and a salty liquid gushes forth beneath his scarf, because he is laughing so hard that he must cry. The air is thin up here, he thinks. Laughing is exerting, he thinks, and stops. Finally, the city. He looks. He sees. He sees his mother running through the garden. Only once, very briefly. Then his father, again and again, with a smile on his face; the wet-nurse; the maid; the gardener. What are all of these people doing in the garden? he asks himself, and then loses himself in the blooming poplars, the cherry trees. He wanders into the southern part of the city, and buys a transistorized radio with his pocket money. His trip has been a clandestine affair to begin with, a long journey and planned long beforehand. The city is alive and crawling with people; the feeling of being tossed to and fro is pleasurable to him, in the same way that later the gigantic octopus with seats and safety bars at the fairgrounds in another world will be pleasurable. Boom-bam this way, boom-bam that way; cheering and shouting; and somewhere in the crowd is his mother, carefree, laughing, cotton candy in hand standing beside her girlfriend, talking about women's things or-something-similar. On top of the snow where he is now sitting and watching himself in the city: mother-perfume, just a hint of it. He smiles. Don't laugh, he thinks, laughing is exerting, the air is too thin. So he wipes away the fairground octopus, his mother and the perfume, and buys himself two more transistorized radios in the bustle below. Once at home he takes them apart and builds them back together again, over and over until they have become receptors once more. One of them he doesn't put together again, but, instead, inserts the wires, connections and coils differently; he reads in books he finds in the father-shelves with the secret drawer in the basement, until he gets it to generate signals and transmit Morse code, and finally he even transmits his voice into the ether. Then his father appearing, finding him there, shocked at what he finds. His father tells him of dangers, of the risk of torture and incarceration, danger to life and limb connected with transmitting codes and voices, he takes the transistor away, and giving his child a worried and reprimanding look, he makes him promise: Never again! I swear! Don't smile, he thinks to himself and searches the city from the top of the mountain. He searches for his cousin. Her kisses, but not only her kisses. He searches for many different things and finds them intact, all of them, finds them the way they were before. They are. They will last, he thinks, but one must climb mountains and become snow blind to taste them again. Nothing prompts his descent. He simply begins, without notice, without a reason. He could just as well have never begun. But now he finds himself standing upright in the wind, still blind, his feet searching for firm ground, facing the direction of the descent. Then he goes down on his knees again. Stay close to the ground, close to the ice, to the cold, his head is tilted to one side, but finally, the city. He searches with his hand. He feels the snow, moves the palm of his hand over it. Finds the pit left by the weight of his body, its outline. He searches. Then he finds it, reaches out for the small transistorized radio and puts it into his coat pocket. You're coming with me, he thinks to himself, and then: Don't smile, smiling is exerting, the air is too thin, and then continues his slippery descent, never losing sight of his goal with his blind eyes. When he, days later, crosses the snowline, he removes the scarf from his head. The skin beneath it has become scurfy. His eyes are pasted shut, purulent. He keeps them closed. His lips are dry, cracked, bloody in places. His fingers, he can't see them, are undoubtedly blue, frostbitten, they are slowly and painfully thawing. Dangerous, he thinks to himself, but they say the symptoms disappear if you immerse them in cold water. Don't stop moving, walk upright now, don't think of your toes. Salt-water helps, he thinks, and tries to cry. His body's own salt to fight puss and scurf. But you have to be sad to be able to cry. He supports himself on the stick he found on the second day of no snow. He has been descending without stopping to sleep. Sleeping is dangerous, he had thought to himself. In the cold you cannot be certain that you will wake up again, and so he had continued on his way, through the unvarying darkness. The stick is a blessing, a blessed-seeing-stick: the path opens up before him and he only falls down on rare occasion now. When he reaches the city limits, he asks for a doctor. People don't seem to be bothered by the fact that he smells bad and is bleeding, that he is blind and speaks with an old-fashioned singsong. They take him by the hand and bring him to a doctor. The doctor asks no questions. Why doesn't the doctor ask any questions? he asks himself, relieved. His eyes are rinsed, his lips treated, his fingers, his toes. The pain gets worse at first, but then it starts to subside.

Some time later he is able to see again, he can stand, he can walk, and he is rested and pays the bill and runs out into the garden. It is hidden beneath a monstrous sky-scraper. He runs south, searching for places where transistorized radios are sold. He finds them. At first he buys only one, then buys himself a bag of candy, then runs back to the radio shop and buys two more. He listens for the new words that have wriggled their way into the old language. Incorporate them, he thinks and he alphabetically sorts through them in his worn vocabulary. He calls his daughter to him, shows her all of his treasures. Later, when the fair comes to town in another world, he will show her how to take them apart and build them back together again, how to turn them into transmitters and receivers. They get lost. They're constantly getting lost in the city. They try to figure out where they should spend the night, and he thinks that a seven-year-old child shouldn't have to think about such things. And so he picks up his daughter, as if she were two or three years old, carries her on his hip, brushes the hair from her brow and searches her eyes. She laughs and pinches his nose. I know, he says, we'll sleep in the desert and his daughter says Ah and Oh and doesn't know what desert means and points to a bearded old man selling marbles. He shakes his head. We're going to the desert now, my dear, he says, and there you don't need any marbles. You need water and a stick, so that you can keep away the tigers and sometimes the lions. They buy a little stick for his daughter, and he uses his larger one for support and slips a water-hose over the right shoulder. It gets cold in the desert at night. That's why it also gets cold in the city at night, the south side, the side facing the desert. That's why it doesn't matter, he says to his daughter, whether we sleep in the city or in the desert, and the little girl points to a boy on a rattling moped whizzing around a corner. The desert night is still and cold, just as he said it would be. It is also bright, and his eyes begin to smart again. First the glistening of the moon, then of the stars. Much too much light, he thinks, it's dangerous, and tightly wraps his scarf around his daughter's temples and begins to sing her a song (a song from the fairgrounds, about octopuses and cotton candy and screaming people riding rollercoasters). He sings to her until she falls asleep. He then puts his dreaming child over his eyes and looks toward the city: the garden, his mother, his father, the wet-nurse, et cetera. And the transistorized radios? Without plucking the child from his eyes, he feels his way to the equipment in his pocket. Everything is still there. Then he hears a tiger creep by. A majestic, stunning, gigantic creature. It's on the prowl. Gazelles, he thinks to himself. They must be bedded down somewhere nearby for the night. Do gazelles bed down for the night? he asks himself. He looks to the city: the maid, the gardener, the poplars, the threat of incarceration, et cetera. Ah yes, and not to forget, the cousin's kisses. Her kisses, of course. Everything is still intact; everything is the way it was before. It is, it remains, he thinks to himself, only one has to spend the night in the desert and put sticks-to-ward-off-tigers next to dunes in order to see it. His child stretches out on his temples and opens her eyes. His daughter gropes for the scarf tied around her head, pulls it off and points to a gazelle prancing around the corner. Do deserts have corners? he asks himself and gives his daughter a nod, and says: That's a gazelle, my dear. The tiger didn't get her tonight.

III – Brand Old

Every place
>   unknown to you
>   is a place
>   and calls you
>> from the outside space
>> inside the world

A dark October day in the northeast (what else?), urgent waiting on the other end of the line, and I listlessly (how else?) agree to give my Yes-or-No as soon as possible. Then I pack my bag, skeptical, halfheartedly, and go, provoked, pushed and prodded by a number of my friends. But I don't go back, I go to a new foreign place.

Every place
>   unknown to you
>   is a place
>   and calls you
>> from the outside space
>> inside the world

and so I start waiting for a call, a space, I start waiting for something to happen. In vain, as it soon turns out, because all the airplane does is take off on time and land on time, and us passengers, all 326 of us, all we do is leave the plane we are on, and then unhurriedly board another (according to schedule and all expectations), and no one calls, and no new space opens up; and I think to myself how frightening it is that here of all places, (again? still?) the schedule always runs like clockwork, to the second, but since this is not in question now, I change planes as calmly as all the others and take pleasure in how smoothly everything goes. Then my bag gets lost. Despite all the calm and punctuality (someone must have made a mistake) the bag doesn't make it from the one plane onto the next, or possibly it (which later I come to know is an erroneous idea), was left inside of the first plane (forgotten deep inside its body like Jonah inside the maw of the whale.) The bag is missing, and with it my book, my note pad, my pen, even my phone. Later: a taxi, a hotel and two phone-calls (the bag arrives during the night), a hotel key and an extra toothbrush. (Jonah may have been deep inside the whale, by the way, but he wasn't forgotten. I'll have to think more, I think to myself, think more about this Jonah, later.)

At first I convince myself that being here is completely absurd (winter boots in southwestern autumn mildness, a spacious sky, colored light, a bustling city, rotunda-shaped thundering traffic, et cetera), but then: I pause for a moment, suddenly. I have experienced this before. My conviction of the complete absurdity of me being here falls from me, as if it had grown too large for me. I have experienced this kind of pausing for a moment before. I have felt it (and it can't have been that long ago) once before, I'm absolutely certain: We fall into each other, the city and me, as if in slow motion, and I see old faces (old: faces from before), and not only faces. The hint of a neighborly smile on a newspaper vendor. A manager's rebuke in the voice of a woman bus driver. The flight of a raven in the beating wings of a seagull up ahead over the square. (No, the light is not golden, and it doesn't smell of dust, nor of jasmine. No, no!) I place one foot in front of the other. I seem to find myself in two (or three? or four?) places at once, as if Teotihuacán were pushing itself out from inside the earth into the architecture of Mexico City, as if a heathen place of worship were to shimmer through the walls of an Italian cathedral upon which it had been built. I ask myself, where I have ended up. (It's on the ticket, I think to myself, and I think this so angrily and so loudly that I am convinced people near me will turn around and look at me.) There is no going back, I murmur to myself, I insist! And now people really do turn around. (That woman, talking to herself, she is.) There is no going back, and this here is not back, this here is southwest. And I run through the walls of my life in the architecture of a new foreign place that has remained familiar to me.

Up until this point, things have been strange, but alright. An imbalance sets in first when you turn the corner. Yet another moment of pause: We fall into each other, and your wife looks from me to you and from you to me and grabs your daughter from your arms and says something I cannot understand, and runs a free hand angrily through her hair and your daughter (that is the daughter whom you've spoken about so tenderly-yet-so-rarely, isn't it?), she points to a fat woman in a screaming yellow sweatshirt selling newspapers (one euro for the newspaper, one euro for herself – or something along those lines), and a youth wearing brand name clothing digs inside his pant pocket and buys himself one. Keep the change, he says, when she wants to hand it to him, and continues on his way.

> Every place
>> unknown to you
>> is a place
>> and calls you
>>> from the outside space
>>> inside the world

but that's wrong, right? Having been provoked, pushed and prodded backfires.

> Every place
>> unknown to me
>> is a place
>> and shoves and heaves me
>>> into the innermost depth
>>> of old geographies

that is what it is, what it does. It shoves me inward, never outward. I fall into myself in foreign places and meet you (for instance) within them, as you're turning a corner, although you shouldn't be here, especially not with wife-and-child, and I ask myself how she knows who I am (if she didn't she wouldn't be yelling that way, or what do you think?), and we're having a hard time catching ourselves as we fall clamping on to each other (this isn't much more than a reflex really), and I see (as if in slow motion) how your eyes are downcast, but then look up again (you want to avert your gaze, and I want you to avert your gaze), but only so that you can sink into mine again, and somewhere a muezzin is crying (a bell is ringing) or maybe it's just the roar of a hungry tiger (who can really know for certain, especially since your wife is making so much noise). Fine, I think to myself, now things have started getting out of hand, and I watch how all kinds of things get into a state of utter disarray (your branding falls onto your daughter's shoulders, you wrap a stick around your temples, your wife rides around us incessantly in a circle on the back of a tiger, et cetera) and I wait, wait until the falling has stopped, this descent, this spinning. (Do you see it too, the puzzle plucked to pieces?) You're nodding (you're nodding?), you raise your head, tearing your gaze out from inside of me, I am relieved, we laugh. Laughing is dangerous, I think to myself, this tiger-woman might become unpleasant and your daughter points at me, she tilts her head to one side and looks up at me. She has eyes-of- dunes. (Did she always have them, or have you showed her the original of her future?) You take the child up into your arms, your wife, confused with wrath, looks from me to you and back, I tie my hair into a ponytail, nod and pass you teotihuacánfar to your right and go to some cathedral and think about Jonah and how he was lost or safe inside that whale, and ask myself why I can only think of this and nothing else right now.

The card arrives after three days (though I discover it much later, nearly four weeks later, on my kitchen table in the northeast, in a neat stack, chronologically sorted by arrival, amongst bills and other mail). On it it says there is no going back. There is the mountain, and there is the desert. It's all still there. Everything, the way it was. And in between, you really should come and take a look at it, in between the masses and the cars and the parks. The city is brand new!

Further down in the corner, squeezed in because you had misjudged how much room you had on the card, it says written in slantways

Every place
    inside of me
    is an exterior place
    and it shoves and heaves me
        into the innermost depth
        of the world's exterior geographies
and I think to myself, Look at that! Maybe one day you'll become a poet after all.

I - Unterhautschmuck

Jeder Ort

> der in mir

> ist

> ein Ort

>> den es nicht gibt

und deine Hand fährt langsam über die Gänsehaut, die sie entlang der Kurve meiner Hüfte verursacht, während du sagst, Ich will dorthin fahren. Mitdir will ich fahren, sagst du, zurück.

Jeder Ort

> der in mir

> ist

> ein Ort

>> den es nicht gibt

>> im Außenraum der Welt

und also sage ich, Was soll ich dort? Was soll dieses Zurück, dieses Mitdir, das heißt: Mitmir?

Im Getümmel eines Flughafens (wo sonst?) streiten wir uns gründlich (wie sonst?). Der Ort, dieser Nichtort, an den du fahren willst, fehlt an vielerlei Stellen. Beispielsweise in Listen, in manchen Listen fehlt er. In anderen nicht. Aber eben beispielsweise in dieser: Mexiko City, Bangkok, Tokio, Dubai, Los Angeles. Ein Listenbeispiel für das Fehlen des Ortes (das streng genommen unmöglich ist, denn wie kann er fehlen, wenn es ihn nicht gibt).

Diesen Ort, auf den wir gebunden, an dem wir zusammengeschweißt sind, den gibt es nicht, denn er ist in mir (woraus zu schließen wäre, daß er mich berührt haben, in mich eingedrungen sein muß, irgendwann einmal vor langer oder kurzer Zeit, aber jedenfalls zu einer gegebenen Zeit, die ihm ausreichend Raum ließ, diesen Von-außen-nach-innen-Wechsel zu vollziehen).

Was es gibt, sind Linien und Muster, feine Striche, Kleckse, Biegungen und Winkel. Zeichen, die er hinterlassen hat aufinmir (woraus zu schließen wäre, daß es ihn, diesen Ort, doch einmal gegeben haben muß oder zumindest gegeben haben könnte, denn wie sonst hätte er sich einprägen können in das, was ich bin?). Unter- und Aufhautschmuckstück, dieser Ort. Branding, Piercing, Signatur. Zeichen, lesbare, unlesbare, die er gelassen hat aufinmir. Aufindir? Tatsächlich. Auch aufindir (weswegen wir innehalten, weswegen wir stehenbleiben beim Bankett im Hotel zwischen all den Gästen, die unsere Rehaugen bewundern und unsere Namen nicht aussprechen können. Unsere Namen, die wir aussprechbar gemacht haben, absprachelos vor Jahren schon, beide, und ohne einander zu kennen. Die wir aussprechbar gemacht haben, um Ansprechbare zu werden).

Heute aber und hier streiten wir uns (selbstverständlich) gründlich im Getümmel eines Flughafens (wo sonst?), und du willst eine Richtung einschlagen, die nicht in mir ist. Zurück gibt es nicht, sage ich.

Wenn ich das tue ..., sagst du und streichst mit dem Blick über meine Lippen und brichst mitten im Satz ab und tauchst zwischen meinen Schlüsselbeinen abwärts, während wir vor dem Bett stehen, noch ganz bekleidet, mit einer rosenfarbenen Hitze unter dem Oliv unserer Gesichter. Wenn ich das tue, sagst du wieder und knetest plötzlich die Finger deiner rechten mit denen deiner linken Hand und reißt deinen Blick von meiner Haut und wirfst ihn in die Büsche hinterm Fenster und wirst blaß, dann gibt es kein Zurück mehr. Kußangst, Folgeangst.

Aber Zurück gibt es ohnehin nicht, das sagte ich doch schon. Mit meinem liniengezeichneten Mund, dem Nichtortbranding an der Schläfe, dem anderen am rechten Brustansatz, noch verdeckt von Spitzen und Seide und dem feinen Baumwollstoff meines Hemdes, sage ich es. Sage, daß es diesen Ort nicht gibt, nicht geben kann: diesen Zurückort, und überzeuge dich für den Moment erst einmal von dem Kuß. Davon, daß es sich lohnt, ihn zu wagen, den Fall aufs Bett, das Entfernen der entfernbaren Häute, das Sichtbarmachen der Narben: Ort-gezeichnet liegen wir in Fernegeographien. Wie ein Magnet hat er uns erst an-, dann aufeinanderprallen lassen, dieser Nichtort, aus dem wir gezeichnet sind. Staunen (heftig, bestürzt) als ich den Berg in deinen Augen taste (im Hotel zwischen all den Gästen, die unsere Rehaugen und Namen undsoweiter), als ich die Wüste in deiner Stimme rieche, am Rand deines Blicks die Kirschblüte schmecke und das Lied vom Taubenschlag in der Bankettluft, kaum daß ich dich zum ersten Male sehe. Ineinanderfallen, sequenzweise, still, die Lider niederschlagen, einmalig, zeitgleich, die Köpfe wenden, lächelfrei: Du? Du also auch? Wie kann das sein? Du – mit deinem liniengezeichneten Mund, dem Branding an der Schläfe und dem anderen am rechten Brustansatz, über das mein Zeigefinger gleitet, wüstenwindfährtig – und ich. Wie konnte das geschehen?

Jeder Ort

    der in mir

    ist

    ein Ort

       den es nicht gibt

       im Außenraum der Welt

und ich bestehe auf seiner Nichtexistenz: In der Welt gehört er der Welt, der Zeit, der Korrosion undsoweiter. In mir ist er eigen. Den Ort, der in mir ist, werde ich nicht vergleichen. Ich werde nicht, und deshalb streiten wir uns gründlich im schütteren Getümmel dieses albernen Provinzflughafens, ich werde nicht den Ort in mir auf seine Kopie im Außen legen. Sie sollen sich ertragen in ihrer Ferne und Nähe, es lernen. Ich erhalte mein (das) Original. Die Differenz interessiert mich nicht. Sie ist. Das reicht. Gleichzeitigkeit der Gesternundheutegeo-graphien in mir und um mich: Deutung bleibt ein mystisches Geschehen.

Es gibt einen Ort, den du Zurück nennst, auf seiner einen Seite ein Berg, auf seiner anderen die Wüste, tagsüber von Sonne beschienen, nachts vom Mond (wenn er nicht neu ist). Töricht ist es, eine Fahrkarte zu kaufen, einen Koffer zu packen, eine Reise zu planen und sich jetzt mit mir darüber zu streiten, daß ich nichtmit-dirkomme. Töricht, wenn ich seit dem ersten Tag Nein sage.

Fahr mit deiner Frau. Sie fährt nicht zurück. Sie fährt in die Zukunft. In etwas, das in ihrer Zukunft ein Original sein wird (für sie). Fahr mit deiner Frau und deinem Kind, wandere herum im Außenbergschatten, grüß nicht von mir (er kennt mich nicht). Fahr du nur. Fahr mit Fraundkind. Fahr morgen oder gestern und laß deine Hand über meinen Körper fahren und nicht nur über und nicht nur deine Hand: Sei in mir. Das gibt es.

Noch eine Weile stehen wir (zwei Stunden nachdem du aus mir auferstanden bist, mir diese Fahrkarte zwischen die Brüste gelegt hast und ein Bild von dem Berg, der in mir ist, den es nicht gibt), stehen im Getümmel am Flughafen (wo sonst?) und streiten uns (natürlich) gründlich. Im Schüttergetümmel der Provinz bist du unglücklich (unglücklich: du kehrst zu deiner Frau zurück, du wirst mitihr reisen, du wirst deinem Kind treu bleiben und ich will, daß du ihm treu bleibst), bin ich unglücklich (unglücklich: Klammerhände rückenverbannt, Blickzwang auf Wasgehtundwasnichtgeht, Stehen, herzscherbenmittig im Regen), streiten wir uns über nicht-existente (zugegeben: ?) Orte. Er ist hier, sage ich, und du stöhnst. Der Ort ist hier, sage ich und zeige auf den Bogen meiner Augenbraue. Deutung: mystisch (was sonst?). Wie konnte es nur geschehen, daß ich neben meinem nun ein weiteres Original dulden muß? Und auch und vor allem: Wie kann es sein, daß du mich brauchst, um dein Original zu erhalten?

Du willst deinen Zurückort als Weiter-, als Fortgang und Wiederbegegnung. Ich will meinen Inmirort als Steinbruch: wo die Erde aufbricht, machtvoll, und gestaltet. Bruchort, an dem es Vorher gibt und Nachher. Steinbruchoriginal: Bewegung durch mein Gesternheute. Das will ich. Das ist.

Hätten wir ein wenig nachgedacht, wir hätten uns das Trugbild erspart, diese Teilbarkeitsillusionen, Ortkongruenzphantasien. Hätten wir auf Lebenswissen gebaut, auf deines, meines, wir hätten die Augen geschlossen, die Finger tasten lassen, meine über dich, deine über mich, wir hätten uns schweigend entkleidet, in Erregung versetzt, hätten gestoßen, gejauchzt, gewimmert, geschnauft, laut aufgestöhnt und hätten die Orte an ihren Orten gelassen. Das wäre klug gewesen: unverblümt und echt. Original wäre es gewesen. Aber wir haben ans Reisen gedacht und ans Nichtreisen mitten im Feiern von Haut und Haar, haben die Brandings an unseren Schläfen verglichen, ihre Ähnlichkeit, ihre nahezu identische Plazierung gefeiert und die Orte in seifigen Goldstaub aus Sehnsucht getaucht. Statt sie zu lassen: Beton, Ziegelstein, Smog, Autos, Massen, Parks, überall große Parks in den Schluchten, natürlich, und die Sache mit der Zeit: Hetzen, Eilen, Uhren. Solche zum Stechen, solche zum Wecken, zum Messen, zum Vergewissern, überall die Sache mit der Zeit, als liefe sie immer geradeaus, immer linear ins Morgen hinüber, und alles, alles so original kopiert wie nur irgend möglich. Wären wir ein wenig mit Bedacht vorgegangen, hätten wir das Ineinanderfallen nur lustwärts genutzt und freudwärts und hätten darauf verzichtet, von Orten, womöglich sogar geteilten, zu faseln, die uns angeblich verbinden, dann müßten wir uns nicht streiten im bergarmen, wüstenleeren, herzzersplitterten Hierjetzt der Lebensgabelung, die auf uns wartet.

Im schütteren Getümmel dieses albernen Pronvinzflughafens, den du nichtohnemich verlassen willst, klingelt (natürlich) dein Telefon in unseren gründlichen Streit hinein. Es ruft dich an deinen Außenort, an dem ich nicht bin und nicht sein werde, den es aber geben muß, denn in mir finde ich ihn nicht, und in dir ist er nicht.

Jeder Ort

    der in mir

    ist

    ein Ort

        den es nicht gibt

und deine Hand drückt auf den Knopf mit der grünen Ikone.

    Jeder Ort

        der in mir

        ist

        ein Ort

            den es nicht gibt

            im Außenraum der Welt

und du sagst, in das kleine silberne Gerät sagst du, Ich sehe dich in zwei Stunden, bin fast schon zurück, bis gleich!, und drückst auf den Knopf mit der kleinen roten Ikone.

II - Blindsehen

Oben. Er liegt ganz oben auf dem Berg. Höher geht nicht ohne Bodenverlust. Der Aufstieg war beschwerlich, hat lange gedauert. Die Brille, Sonnenbrille, hat er vergessen, weswegen er kaum noch etwas sieht. Schneeblind. Das ist gefährlich, denkt er, aber man sagt, daß es sich wieder legt, wenn das Weiß fort ist. Das Schneeweiß, Gletscherweiß, meint er, von dem er umgeben ist seit Tagen, seit er, als er die Schneegrenze erreichte, doch nicht umkehrte, sondern weiterlief. Hoch, einfach immer weiter nach oben. In Schlangenlinien, abgrundnah zeitweise, quer über Hochplateaus und immer auf knirschendem, blendendem Weiß. Einem Weiß, von dem er feststellen mußte, daß es in Wirklichkeit gar nicht weiß ist. Wenn er es anhob, wenn er die Hand in eine Schneewehe tauchte, sie zur Schale formte und die Himmelskristalle nah an die Augen hielt. Blau entdeckte er in ihnen. Grau auch und Grün. Rot fand sich, Braun, Gelb ohnehin, und als schließlich auch noch Schwarz auftauchte, war er still geworden tief unten, innen. Da, wo Gedankenrauschen und Fühlflüsse stetes Klingen erzeugen, da war eine Stille ausgebrochen in ihm, und er hatte sich hingesetzt. Mitten in die schräge, gleißende Eiswüste hatte er sich gesetzt, sich dem Staunen hingegeben und nach Versatzstücken aus dem lang zurückliegenden Physikunterricht geangelt, Optik, Farbenlehre, aber nichts Sinnvolles mehr zusammenbekommen.

Später, schon gipfelnah, hatte das Schwarz überhandgenommen, hatte es die restlichen Farben verschluckt und von der Welt war nur noch ihr Dunkel geblieben. Das ist gefährlich, dachte er, aber man sagt, daß es sich wieder legt, wenn das Weiß fort ist. Inzwischen kroch er auf allen Vieren übers Eis, über scharfe Kanten und immer noch an Abgründen vorbei. Aufrecht gehen ist nicht mehr, dachte er, ist nicht mehr sicher, also sinnvoll. Bodennah bleiben, eisnah, weißnah. Und dann griff er ins Leere. Griff wieder und wieder und fand nach kurzem, ebenem

Tasten, nur noch Abfallendes auf der anderen Seite: oben. Er ist jetzt ganz oben auf dem Berg. Höher geht nicht ohne Bodenverlust, denkt er und weiß hinter sich, weit unten die Stadt, läßt sich fallen, breit auf den Bauch, die Brust, die Schenkel, läßt das Gesicht in Eisschnee tauchen, kalt, fast erfroren, blind ohnehin, und horcht. Wind. Natürlich. Dann noch: Wind und Wind. Sonst absolut nichts. Oder Stille vielleicht. Windstille, wenn man so will, denkt er und lächelt in atemschmelzende Schneekristalle. Er dreht sich auf den Rücken, schiebt sich in halbes, in ellbogengestütztes Sitzen hoch und sucht mit dem Blick die Stadt. Dunkel. Grauschlierige Schatten, Schmerzstiche, ein Tränen an den Augenrändern, an einer Stelle (irgendwie tief innen im Auge?), von der er bis gestern nicht wußte, daß es sie gibt. Seit sie sticht und brennt und Zacken in sein Gehirn gräbt, kennt er sie. Netzhaut, vermutet er, greift nach seinem Schal und bindet ihn über die Augen fest um den Kopf. Bloß nicht ablösen, denkt er, das darf sie auf keinen Fall, sich ablösen. Das ließe sich schließlich nicht rückgängig machen. Jedenfalls nicht mehr nach all den Tagen des Abstiegs, die ihm noch bevorstehen. Vermutlich zumindest. Falls er es sich nicht anders überlegt. Aber dann brauchte er auch die Netzhaut nicht mehr. Für den Moment also deshalb doch lieber der Schal, der angenehme, warme Druck an den Schläfen, die Außendunkelheit, die sich vor die Welthelligkeit schiebt, die den Innenschmerz lindert. Handlungsspielräume, denkt er. Man muß sich Handlungsspielräume offen halten, Wahlen schaffen, Wahlen, denkt er langsam zu Ende, und denkt an den serpentinengezeichneten Abstieg, steil, aufregend, gefährlich, mit schließlich wiederkehrendem Augenlicht, und dann denkt er daran, wie er hier liegt und einschläft und der Abstieg unter ihm ohne ihn vonstatten geht und er sich nicht die Mühe machen muß, noch einmal aufzustehen, zu tasten, zu sehen, die Netzhaut am hinteren Augengrund zu halten undsoweiter, und setzt sich richtig, setzt sich vorerst endgültig auf. Jetzt also die Stadt. Deshalb ist er schließlich hier. Wegen der Stadt. Das Ziel nicht aus den Augen verlieren, denkt er und lächelt schon wieder, diesmal in die Kondensstreifen von Atemluft vor seinem sonnenverbrannten Gesicht. Das Ziel also schön im Auge behalten, denkt er, kann sich nicht verkneifen, selbst über die Wiederholung, die abgewandelte, zu lächeln, lächeln, lächeln, bis er mit einem Mal lauthals auflacht und salzige Flüssigkeit unter dem Schal hervorquillt, weil er vor lauter Lachen weinen muß. Die Luft ist dünn hier oben, denkt er. Lachen strengt an, denkt er und hört wieder auf damit. Jetzt also die Stadt. Er schaut. Er sieht. Sieht seine Mutter durch den Garten laufen. Nur einmal, sehr kurz. Dann den Vater, immer wieder, mit einem Lächeln im Gesicht, die Amme, die Putzfrau, den Gärtner. Was machen die alle im Garten? fragt er sich und verliert sich im Blühen der Pappeln, der Kirschen. Er wandert in den Süden der Stadt, kauft Transistorradios vom Taschengeld. Erst nur eines. Der Ausflug ist ohnehin ein heimlicher, ein langer auch und von langer Hand vorbereitet. Die Stadt wuselt und wimmelt und schleudert ihn genußvoll hin und her wie später die riesenhafte Krake mit Sitzplätzen und Sicherheitsgestänge auf dem Jahrmarkt in einer anderen Welt. Rums hierhin, bums dahin, mit Jauchzen und Schreien und irgendwo im Gewimmel steht die Mutter, sorglos, lachend, mit Zuckerwatte neben der Freundin und redet Frauensachen odersoähnlich. Überm Schnee, wo er sitzt und sich in der Stadt betrachtet, überm Schnee Mutterparfum, eine Ahnung nur. Er lächelt. Nicht lachen, denkt er, Lachen ist anstrengend, die Luft ist zu dünn. Also wischt er die Jahrmarktskrake fort, die Mutter und das Parfum und kauft doch noch zwei Transistorradios im Getümmel unten. Zu Hause nimmt er sie auseinander und baut sie wieder zusammen, so lange, bis sie erneut zu Empfängern geworden sind. Eines läßt er geöffnet, steckt Drähte, Verbindungen, Spulen um, schlägt in Büchern nach aus dem Vaterregal im Keller, aus dem mit Geheimfach, so lange, bis es sendet, bis es Zeichen morst und schließlich, Tage später, sogar seine Stimme in den Äther schickt. Dann der Vater, wie er plötzlich im Zimmer steht, wie er ihn findet, erschrickt. Der Vater erzählt von Gefahren, von Folter-, Gefängnis- und Lebensgefahren, die mit dem Senden von Zeichen, von Stimmen einhergehen, nimmt ihm den Sender weg, mit strafend-besorgtem Blick auf sein Kind, läßt ihn ver- sprechen: Nie wieder, nie wieder, ich schwöre! Nicht lächeln, denkt er und sucht von oben weiter in der Stadt herum. Sucht nach der Cousine. Nach ihren Küssen und nicht nur ihren Küssen. Nach allerlei sonst und findet die Dinge, unangetastet, alle, so wie sie waren. Sie sind. Sie bleiben, denkt er, nur daß man Berge besteigen, schnee- blind werden muß, um sie wieder zu schmecken. Es gibt keinen Anlaß für den Abstieg. Er beginnt einfach, unangekündigt, sinnfrei. Genausogut hätte er ausbleiben können. Aber jetzt findet er sich aufrecht im Wind, blind immer noch, tastend mit den Füßen nach festem Grund und abwärtsgerichtet. Dann geht er wieder auf die Knie. Bodennah bleiben, eis-, kältenah, schräg kopfunter zurück in die Stadt. Er tastet. Mit der flachen Hand fährt er über den Schnee. Die Kuhle, die das Gewicht seines Körpers gedrückt hat, ihre Ränder. Er sucht. Dann hat er es, greift nach dem kleinen Sender, dem verbotenen, gefängnisgefährlichen Nichtmehrtransistorradio und steckt es in die Jackentasche. Du kommst mit, denkt er und: Nicht lächeln, lächeln ist anstrengend, die Luft ist zu dünn, und schlid- dert langsam weiter, das Ziel vor den blinden Augen. Als er die Schneegrenze überschreitet, Tage später, nimmt er den Schal vom Kopf. Die Haut darunter ist schorfig geworden. Die Augen verklebt, eitrig. Er hält sie geschlossen. Die Lippen trocken, gesprungen, blutig an vielen Stellen. Die Finger, unsichtbar, aber deutlich blau, gefroren. Sie tauen schmerzhaft wieder auf. Gefährlich, denkt er, aber man sagt, daß es vergeht, wenn man sie in kaltes Wasser taucht. Weitergehen, aufrecht inzwischen, nicht an die Zehen denken. Salzwasser hilft, denkt er und versucht zu weinen. Körpersalz gegen Eiter und Schorf. Aber zum Weinen muß man traurig sein. Er stützt sich auf einen Stock, den er am zweiten schneefreien Morgen fand. Den Abstieg durch den Schnee hat er schlaflos vollzogen. Schlafen ist gefährlich, hat er gedacht. Man wacht nicht mehr auf in der Kälte, und war weitergewandert durch immer gleiches Dunkel. Der Stock ist ein Segen, Sehsegenstock: Der Weg tut sich vor ihm auf, und er fällt nur noch selten. Als er an die Stadtgrenze kommt, fragt er nach einem Arzt. Es scheint die Leute nicht zu stören, daß er stinkt und blutet, blind ist und in einem altmodischen Singsang spricht. Sie nehmen ihn bei der Hand und führen ihn zum Arzt. Der Arzt stellt keine Fragen. Warum stellt der Arzt keine Fragen?, fragt er sich beruhigt. Die Augen werden gewaschen, die Lippen behandelt, die Finger, die Zehen. Die Schmerzen werden erst stärker, dann schwächer. Irgendwann sieht er wieder, steht, geht er wieder, hat er ausgeschlafen, bezahlt die Rechnung und läuft zum Gar- ten. Der liegt verborgen unter einem Hochhausungetüm. Er läuft in den Süden, sucht Transistorradioständе. Findet sie. Er kauft erst eines, geht, kauft eine Tüte Naschzeug, läuft zurück zum Radiostand und kauft noch zwei. Er lauscht auf die neuen Worte, die sich in die alte Sprache gewunden haben. Einverleiben, denkt er und sortiert sie alphabetisch in sein abgenutztes Vokabular. Er ruft seine Tochter, führt ihr seine Schätze vor. Später, jahrmarktnah, wird er ihr zeigen, wie man sie auseinander- und wieder zusammenbaut, wie man Sender aus ihnen macht und Empfänger. Sie verlaufen sich. Ständig verlaufen sie sich in der Stadt. Sie überlegen, wo sie übernachten sollen, und er denkt, daß ein Kind von sieben Jahren in solche Überlegungen nicht einbezogen werden sollte. Also nimmt er die Tochter auf den Arm. Als wäre sie zwei oder drei, hält er, trägt er sie auf der Hüfte, schiebt ihr Haare aus der Stirn und sucht in ihren Augen herum. Sie lacht und zwickt ihn in die Nase. Ich hab's, sagt er, wir schlafen in der Wüste, und seine Tochter macht Ah und Oh und weiß nicht, was Wüste heißt, und zeigt auf einen bärtigen Alten, der Murmeln verkauft. Er schüttelt den Kopf. Wir gehen jetzt in die Wüste, mein Herz, sagt er, da braucht man keine Murmeln. Wasser braucht man und einen Stock, um die Tiger zu vertreiben oder manchmal die Löwen. Sie kaufen einen kleinen Stock für die Tochter, er stützt sich auf seinen großen und hängt sich einen Wasserschlauch über die rechte Schulter. In der Wüste wird es nachts kalt. Deshalb wird es auch in der Stadt nachts kalt, an ihrem Südende, Wüstenende. Deshalb ist es auch egal, sagt er zu seiner Tochter, ob wir nun in der Stadt schlafen oder in der Wüste, und die Kleine zeigt auf einen Jungen, der auf einem knatterndem Moped um die Ecke saust. Die Wüstennacht ist still und kalt, wie er es vorausgesagt hat. Hell ist sie auch, und seine Augen beginnen wieder zu schmerzen. Gleißendes, erst vom Mond, später von den Sternen. Viel zuviel Licht, denkt er, das ist gefährlich, und wickelt seiner Tochter den Schal fest um die Schläfen und singt ihr ein Lied (ein Jahrmarktslied mit Kraken und Zuckerwatte und johlenden Achterbahnmenschen), singt ihr ein Lied, bis sie schläft. Dann legt er sich das träumende Kind über die Augen und sieht nach der Stadt: der Garten, die Mutter, der Vater, die Amme undsoweiter. Die Transistorradios? Ohne sich das Kind von den Augen zu klauben, tastet er nach den Geräten in seiner Tasche. Alles noch da. Dann hört er einen Tiger vorbeischleichen. Das Tier ist gigantisch und von atemraubender Eleganz. Es hat die Witterung aufgenommen. Gazellen, denkt er. Ganz in der Nähe müssen Gazellen ihr Nachtlager aufgeschlagen haben. Schlagen Gazellen Nachtlager auf? fragt er sich. Dann sieht er wieder nach der Stadt: die Putzfrau, der Gärtner, die Pappeln, das Gefängnis undsoweiter. Ach ja, die Cousinenküsse, die auch, natürlich. Alles unangetastet, alles so, wie es war. Es ist, es bleibt, denkt er, nur daß man in der Wüste übernachten muß und Tigerstöcke neben Dünen legen, um es zu sehen. Auf seinen Schläfen räkelt sich das Kind und schlägt die Augen auf. Seine Tochter tastet nach dem Schal um ihren Kopf, zieht ihn fort und zeigt auf eine Gazelle, die eben um die Ecke läuft. Gibt es in der Wüste Ecken? fragt er sich und nickt seiner Tochter zu und sagt: Das ist eine Gazelle, Liebes. Der Tiger hat sie heut nacht nicht erwischt.

III - Brandalt

Jeder Ort
    den du nicht kennst
   ist
    ein Ort
      der dich ruft
      in den Außenraum der Welt

Trüber Nordostoktober (was sonst?), ein dringliches Warten am anderen Ende der Leitung und ich verspreche lustlos (wie sonst?) ein baldiges Jaodernein. Dann packe ich meine Koffer, unüberzeugt, halbherzig, und fahre, getrieben von gut geratenen Schlägen aus dem Freundeskreis, nicht zurück, fahre in eine neue Fremde.

    Jeder Ort

        den du nicht kennst

        ist

        ein Ort

            der dich ruft

            in den Außenraum der Welt

und also warte ich auf ein Rufen, einen Raum, darauf, daß etwas geschieht.

    Vergeblich, wie sich bald zeigt, denn das Flugzeug hebt einfach nur pünktlich ab und landet pünktlich, und wir alle, dreihundertsechsundzwanzig Passagiere, steigen hastlos um von einem Flieger in den nächsten (wie geplant und erwartet), und niemand ruft, und kein Raum tut sich auf und gar nichts und ich denke, wie beängstigend es ist, daß ausgerechnet hier die Fahrpläne immer (wieder? noch?) so am Schnürchen laufen, so auf die Sekunde genau eingehalten werden, aber weil das ein Nebenschauplatz ist, steige ich friedlich um mit all den anderen und genieße den reibungslosen Ablauf der Dinge.

    Dann bleibt der Koffer auf der Strecke. Trotz all der Ruhe und Pünktlichkeit ist er (jemand muß sich vertan haben) aus dem einen Flieger nicht in den anderen getragen worden (oder vielleicht ist er gar, aber das stellt sich später als irrige Annahme heraus, gar nicht aus dem ersten herausgeholt, sondern tief in seinem Bauch vergessen worden, wie Jonas im Wal). Der Koffer also bleibt auf der Strecke und mit ihm das Buch, das Heft, der Stift, sogar das Telefon. Später ein Taxi, ein Hotel, drei nette Angestellte, zwei Anrufe (der Koffer kommt in der Nacht und mit ihm das Buch, das Heft undsoweiter), ein Zimmerschlüssel, eine Ersatzzahnbürste. (Im übrigen war Jonas zwar tief im Wal, aber keineswegs vergessen. Weiterdenken, denke ich, an diesem Jonas weiterdenken, später.)

    Für den Moment überzeuge ich mich erst einmal von der Absurdität meines Hierseins (Winterstiefel in südwestlichem Herbstlau, hoher Himmel, farbige Lichter, heftiges Straßenleben, rotundengebogen brüllender Verkehr undsoweiter), aber dann: Innehalten, plötzlich. Ich kenne es. Die Absurditätsüberzeugung fällt von mir ab wie zu groß Geratenes. Dieses Innehalten kenne ich. Ich habe es (und das kann noch nicht lange her sein) schon einmal erlebt, da bin ich mir sicher: Ich falle in die Stadt. Wir fallen (so nämlich viel treffender) ineinander, die Stadt und ich, wie in Zeitlupe, und ich sehe alte Gesichter (alt: Gesichter von früher) – und nicht nur Gesichter. Ein Nachbarslächeln um den Mund des Zeitungsverkäufers. Ein Direktorenverweis in der Stimme der Busfahrerin. Ein Rabenflug im Schwingenschlag der Möwe weiter vorn überm Platz. (Nein, das Licht ist nicht goldfarben, und es riecht hier weder nach Staub, noch nach Jasmin. Nein, nein!) Ich frage mich, wo ich hier gelandet bin, setze einen Fuß vor den nächsten. Als schöbe sich Teotihuacán aus der Erde hoch in die Architektur von Mexiko Stadt, als schimmerte im Gemäuer eines italienischen Doms, die heidnische Kultstätte, auf der er errichtet wurde, finde ich mich an zwei (oder drei? vier?) Orten gleichzeitig wieder. Ich frage mich, wo ich hier bin. (Steht auf dem Fahrschein, denke ich und denke es so ärgerlich und laut, daß ich meine, die Leute müßten sich nach mir umsehen.) Zurück gibt es nicht, murmele ich vor mich hin, darauf bestehe ich! Und jetzt sehen sich die Leute tatsächlich um. (Redet mit sich selbst, die Frau.) Zurück gibt es nicht, und hier ist nicht Zurück, hier ist Südwesten. Ich frage mich, wo ich gelandet bin, und laufe durch das Gemäuer meines Lebens in dieser bekanntgebliebenen Architektur einer neuen Fremde.

Bis hier hin sind die Dinge zwar eigenartig, aber in Ordnung. Aus dem Lot geraten sie erst, als du um die Ecke läufst. Innehalten, wieder, wie damals und wie mit dieser Stadt gerade eben: Wir fallen ineinander, und deine Frau sieht von mir zu dir und von dir zu mir und reißt dir die Tochter aus dem Arm und sagt etwas, aber ich verstehe nicht was, und fährt sich mit der freien Hand wütend durch die Haare, und deine Tochter (ist das deine Tochter, von der du sowenigsoinnig erzählt hast?) deine Tochter zeigt auf eine dicke Frau in quietschgelbem Sweatshirt, die eine Zeitung verkauft (ein Euro für die Zeitung, ein Euro für sie – oder so in etwa zumindest), und ein Jugendlicher in Markenklamotten greift in die Hosentasche und kauft sich eine. Stimmt so, sagt er, als die Verkäuferin ihm das Wechselgeld hinhält, und geht weiter.

Jeder Ort

    den du nicht kennst

    ist

    ein Ort

        der dich ruft

        in den Außenraum der Welt

aber das stimmt nicht, nicht wahr? Die gut geratenen Schläge aus dem Freundeskreis gehen nach hinten los.

Jeder Ort

    den ich nicht kenne

    ist

    ein Ort

        der mich stößt und wuchtet

        innenraumtief

        in alte Geographien

das ist es, was er tut. Er stößt mich nach innen, keineswegs nach Außen.

Ich falle in mich hinein an unbekannten Orten und treffe in ihnen (zum Beispiel) dich, wie du um eine Ecke biegst, obwohl du nicht hier sein solltest, schon gar nicht mit Frauundkind, und ich frage mich, woher sie weiß, wer ich bin (sonst würde sie ja nicht so schimpfen oder wie siehst du das?), und wir haben Mühe, uns zurecht-zufinden im Fall und uns dabei nicht aneinander zu klammern (was im Grunde nicht viel mehr als ein Reflex ist), und ich sehe (in Zeitlupe), wie du die Augen erst niederschlägst, sie dann wieder aufschlägst (du willst deinen Blick abwenden, und ich will, daß du deinen Blick abwendest), aber doch nur, um noch einmal in meinen zu versinken, und irgendwo ruft ein Muezzin (läutet eine Glocke) oder vielleicht ist es auch das Brüllen eines hungrigen Tigers (wer kann das schon so genau sagen, vor allem, wo deine Frau so viel Krach macht).

Also gut, denke ich, jetzt sind die Dinge aus dem Lot geraten, und sehe zu, wie alles mögliche durcheinander purzelt (das Branding fällt deiner Tochter auf die Schulter, du wickelst dir einen Stock um die Schläfen, deine Frau reitet, immer im Kreis, auf dem Tiger um uns herum undsoweiter) und warte, bis das Fallen zu Ende ist, die Abwärtsbewegung, das Trudeln. (Siehst du es auch, das zerpflückte Puzzle?) Du nickst (du nickst?), hebst ruckartig den Kopf, reißt deinen Blick aus mir heraus, ich atme auf, wir lachen. Lachen ist gefährlich, denke ich, diese Tigerfrau könnte ausfallend werden, und deine Tochter zeigt auf mich, legt den Kopf schief und sieht zu mir hoch. Sie hat Dünenaugen. (Hatte sie die schon immer oder hast du ihr das Original ihrer Zukunft gezeigt?) Du nimmst dein Kind in den Arm, deine Frau sieht wutverwirrt von mir zu dir und wieder zurück, ich binde mir die Haare hinterm Kopf zu einem Zopf, nicke und gehe teotihuacánweit rechts an dir vorbei zu irgendeinem Dom und denke nach über Jonas' Walverlorenheit oder Walgeborgenheit, und frage mich, warum ich nur daran und an nichts anderes denken kann in diesem Moment.

Die Karte kommt nach drei Tagen (auch wenn ich selbst sie erst viel später, nämlich ungefähr vier Wochen später, auf meinem Nordostküchentisch finde, sorgsam chronologisch nach dem Datum des Eintreffens zwischen Rechnungen und sonstige Post sortiert).

Zurück gibt es nicht, steht darauf. Den Berg gibt es und die Wüste. Es ist alles noch da. Alles wie immer. Und dazwischen, das solltest du dir wirklich mal ansehen, dazwischen Massen und Autos und Parks. Die Stadt ist brandneu!

Weiter unten am Rand, ein wenig gequetscht, weil du dich mit dem knappen Kartenraum verschätzt hast, steht angeschrägt

Jeder Ort

    der in mir

    ist

    außer mir und

        stößt und wuchtet mich

        innenraumtief

        in Außenraumgeographien der Welt

und ich denke, Sieh an! Vielleicht wird eines Tages doch noch ein Dichter aus dir.

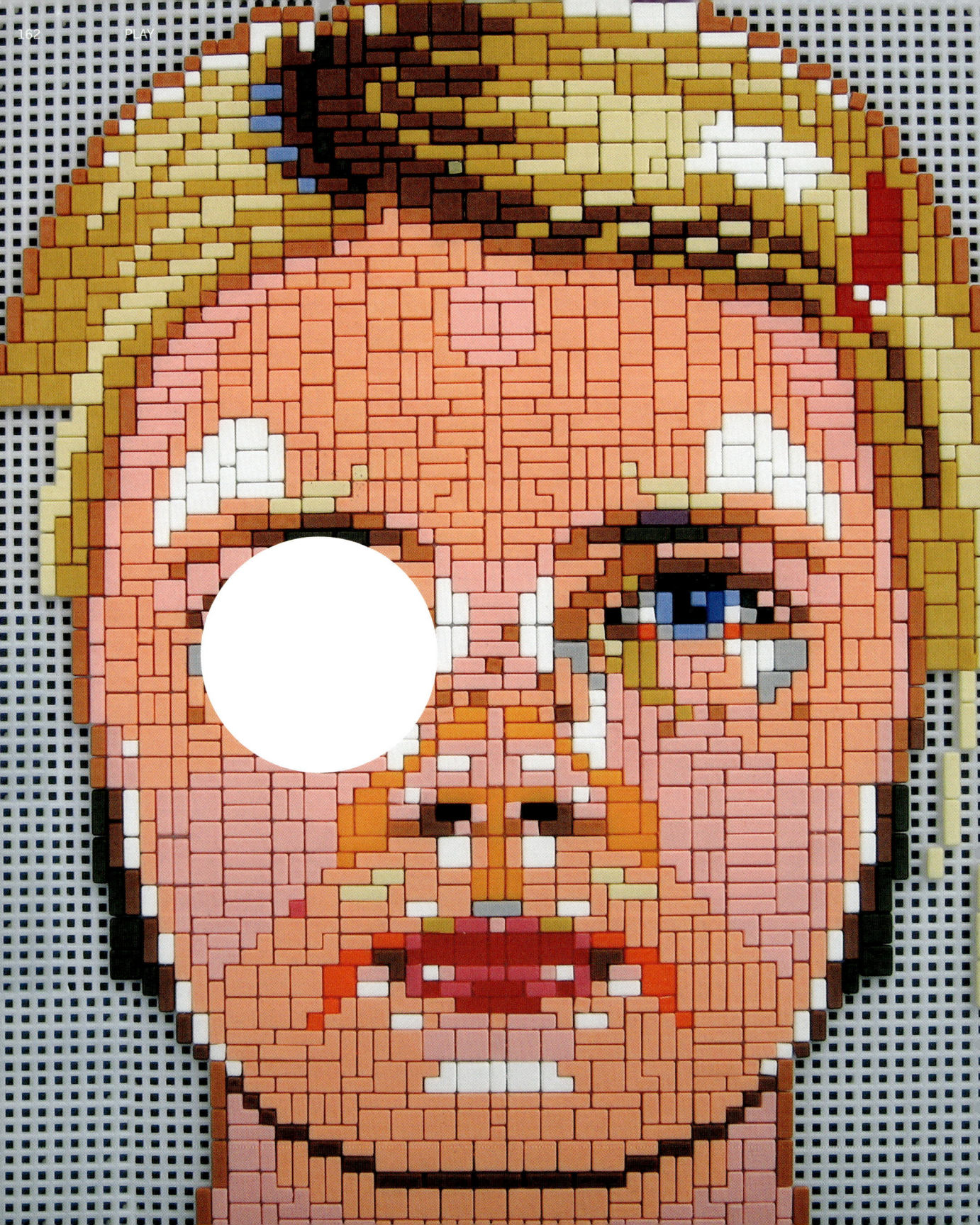

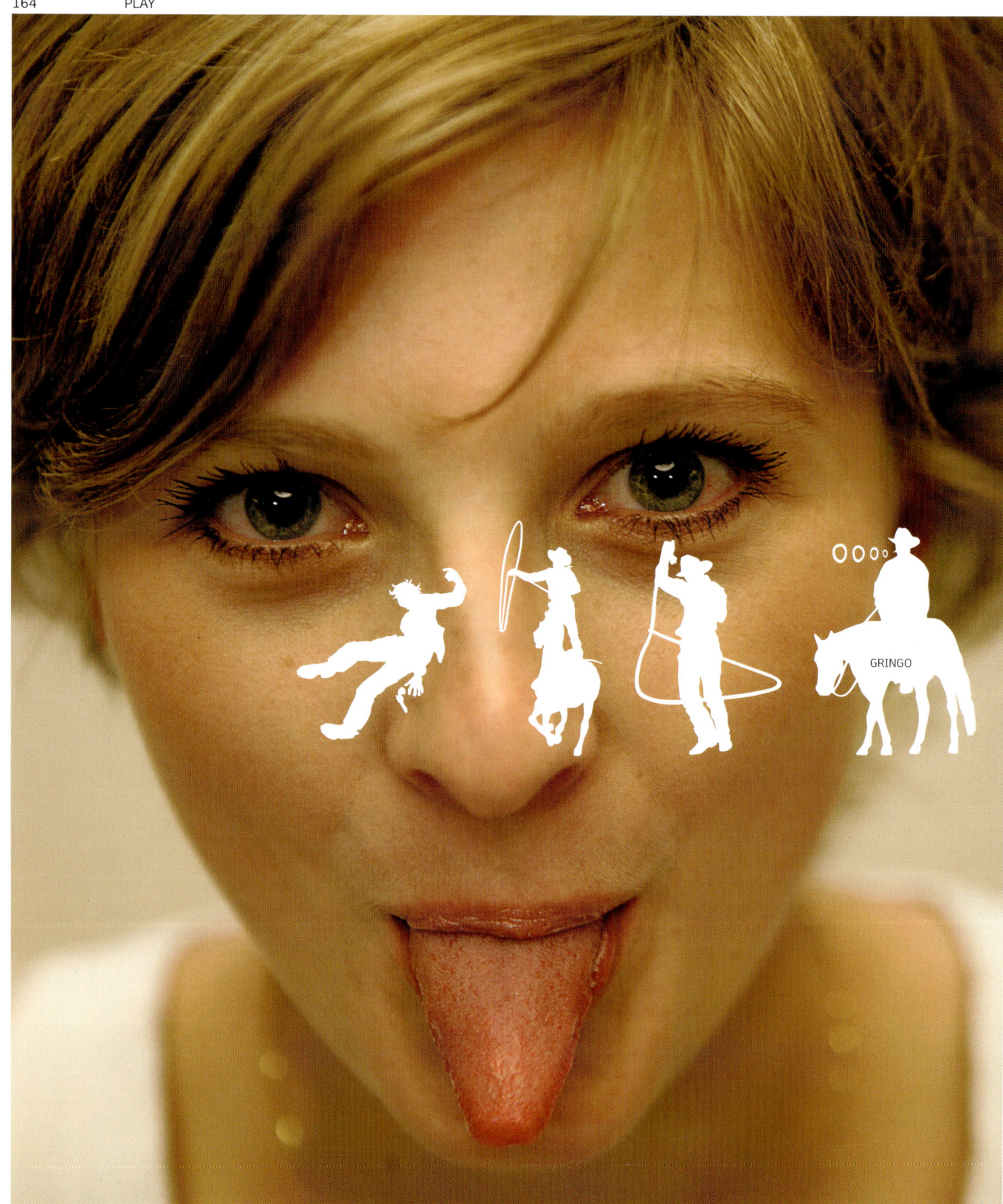

GRINGO

Shooting: It is important to have good gun skills.
The more you practice shooting, the better you should become.

Control: To be „Large and In Charge" will require
you to control the field with shock and awe. If you
are not shooting at something, then you are not
overcompensating in the shooting category.

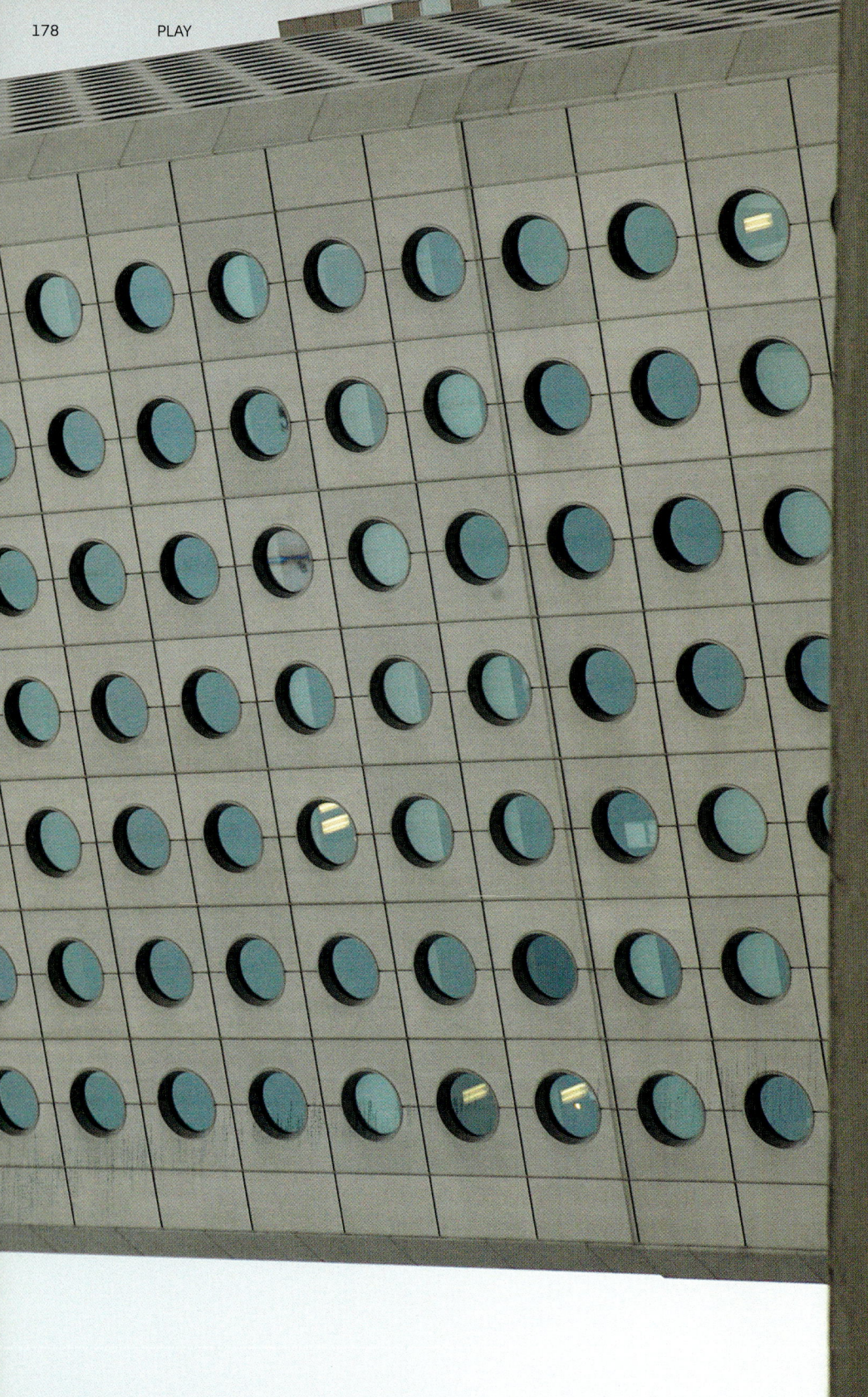

CLONING GODS, READING BAR CODES

DISCONTINUITY IN PRESENT-DAY INDIA

POEMS

ILIJA MARINOW TROJANOW

for chotabhai

kumbha mela 2001. it is a cold morning yet undiscovered by the resilient winter sun. a pit littered with chai cups, some made of plastic, now crushed and crumpled, others made of clay, already dissolving under the dew. old and new lie next to one another, mixed and intermingled; the ancient is about to pass away, while the modern is geared for eternity, or at least for a kalpa which seems to us eternal. plastic is of a pure impurity. before use it looks as clean as it can get, but a heap of plastic (bisleri bottles, pepsi cups) by the side of the path seems like eternal pollution, without hope of a redeeming purification. the introduction of plastic cups at the kumbh mela, or for that matter at nearly every railway station in the country, is a radical discontinuity.

today's india (asia, the world) is a discontinuous system, as complex as the latest microsoft operational software, on the verge of the dysfunctional with any given combination of commands and processes, but functioning nevertheless. on the verge of the incomprehensible. defining and refining identity on a daily basis. discontinuity is a central issue in public discourse, in political combat, instrumentalized by people with a 19th century mindset, who believe that the continuous is still an option for us to choose. they – be it hindutva propagandists, shiv sena warriors, vernacular language authors or marxist backwaterists – demonise discontinuity in order to put the blame on an enemy with an invented and projected homogenic identity, be it islam, the western world, the english language or globalisation. the parameters of this combat are one-dimensional and linear, but the combat is held in a system of discontinuity. It is as if you are introducing an abacus into ms-dos.

maha kumbh mela january 2001. the confluence of ganga and jamna. brown waters blue waters have mixed for a very long time, as have beliefs, songs, stories. every twelve years spirituality meets reality on a massive scale, and by now reality means commerce means technology. huge video screens welcome the kalpvasi to the land of amul and rexona (imagine the two million assembled sadhus all using deodorants). the ongoing ads are the undercurrent to the orgiastic frenzy of ritual, of puja, yagna and snaan. they play the role of the underscored information on the news channels, be it cnn or cnbc. while an activist from some ngo is being interviewed, the undercurrent draws your attention to the nasdaq and the dax and the nikkei and the bse. asian paints 295.30 castrol india 199.90 punjab tractors 170.85 the flow is determined by the under-current, as we all know. madras cements 4350 nagarjuna fertilisers 6.10. the ngo activist is a beautiful bird perched on driftwood, flowing down the ganga, a delight and comfort to the eye, but of little relevance to the stream of things. pritish nandy communications 38.80.

this undercurrent is global. philips 98,30. a pure import, in earlier days called colonialism.

cadbury 491,90 the bombay stock exchange is a mechanism of international efficiency. gilette 365,75 throw a trader from hongkong onto the floor, give him an hour or so to set his sights and he will be dealing with homely delight. procter & gamble 475,95 no cultural bias here, no traditions, no elements of the village market of the city bazaar. with one exception. trading on the bse is 90% day trading. and day trading is purely speculative. infosys 3790,15 it is prone to collusion, manipulation and front-running. private side-deals are easily made. rayban 54,55 a few people can control the trading and the trading is in a state of nearly perfect lawlessness. no one gets caught, no one gets punished. a case or two aside. kodak 207,05 this system of easy gratification needs to be preserved. So it might be defined as TRADITION, as CORE VALUES, as OURS. then this undercurrent, this reality, can not be opposed. nestle 504,25 even ten years after the begin of liberalisation it is extremely cumbersome for a foreigner to enter the bse and the indian stock market. it might take you two days to get accredited in taiwan and a week in south korea, but in india you will struggle for anything between six weeks and six months. But the international investors are knocking at the gates, the last fortress of purely indigenous power will soon fall. siemens 257,75

the sangam of maha kumbh mela january 29, 2001. juna akhara, the most militant of akharas (an order of sadhus, a thousand years old), occupies the beach, with a hard drumming beat and thousand naked feet. after the bath the naga sadhus swing swords, their wet skin glistening in the morning sun. one of the brigade snatches the camera of a foreign journalist and throws it onto the ground, spearing it with a trishul like a demon. a comrade accompanies him in an ecstatic dance over the conquered camera. on the other side of the beach a dressed sadhu catches everything on betacam. for posterity? for the in-house movie evening at the ashram? other sadhus are modelling, climbing a fence, posing, showing off their muscles like bodybuilders in a show. they shower the assembled photographers with abuse and vulgar gestures. a policeman throws stones at the photographers. a sadhu throws pebbles at the policeman. there is panic amongst the naked and the dressed, as the sadhus make their way back to camp. an army of saints bridges the ganga.

what is the undercurrent?

where are the banks of the river?

a day's trip down-river, in varanasi , a man called mahantji mishra is trying to save the ganges. as a believer, he says, i have to have my daily snaan in ganga mataji. as a scientist, a professor of engineering, i would not even put my toe into this filthy river. life is like a stream, he says, one bank is the vedas, the other bank is the modern world with all its science and technology. if both banks are not firm, the water will scatter. if they hold, the river will run its course. a surprising metaphor from somebody who has lived all his life at the banks of the ganges. for this river is a master of discontinuity. it changes its course constantly, it floods and it recedes, it scatters its blessings. creation and invention are no longer two opposing banks, two separate realities. carrots are a human invention (the wild carrot, daucus carota, is a insipid weed. the famous har-ki-pauri ghat in haridwar is on the banks of a canal, not on the ganga itself! geologists and climatologists foresee the end of ganga because of the melting of the glaciers in the himalayas. other scientists say that the global warming will help us survive for a while longer as the next ice period is around the corner. remember the vedas: the death of ganga foretold. when it becomes overburdened by sin, before the end of kaliyuga.

the kumbh mela is a gigantic web without a spider. webs or nets are ancient concepts of inter-dependency, conceived well ahead of the chaos theory. the net of indra, the world as a web, every being a knot therein, that was an early buddhist idea. there was advaita and other similar philosophies. even late-comers like teilhard de chardin envisioned a collective consciousness. spiritual concepts have materialised thanks to technology: the internet, the most obvious, but also the net of global economy, cyberspace and the deciphering of the dna-structure, spiritually foretold by the buddhist understanding that the individual is made up of non-individual elements. networking is the new method of empowering. no one at the kumbh mela understood this better than muniji, the head of the parmarth niketan ashram in rishikesh, who was more effective than millions of kalpvasi lumped together into a mass – in a discontinuous system masses are impressive in size, but weak in influence. muniji met the bbc, muniji chaired a conference of western ecologists concerned about the ganga, muniji celebrated aarti together with ashok singhal and the dalai lama (who splashed water at the photographers, laughing, seemingly saying: i know it is all a game). muniji has his american jewish secretary send out monthly emails informing those interested about the itinerary and the worldly abodes of mahant maharaja muniji, cybering between the usa and taiwan and japan and france and the cities of india, but spiritually always in touch with the flow of ganga.

the bar code is the closest humanity has come to the net of indra. 5dash099706dash56802 5dash. Esperanto was an artificial language, developed by a polish humanist to unite mankind by enabling communication between everyone. 9dash788190dash113205dash. in the 21st century esperanto is a losing venture. the bar code is more efficient than esperanto, the bar code is completely cultureless and timeless, and completely comprehensible. we guarantee there will be no misunderstandings. 4dash477739dash378409dash. should the current 13 digits not suffice, the overpopulation of products will only be a mathematical challenge.

in the europe of modernity, god was killed. in the india of post-liberalisation, the gods are cloned. cloning is the ultimate preservation of the status quo. it is more effective than the caste system. god is decontextualised, desocialised, completely individualised, another victim of the manipulative powers of the privileged, who themselves prefer to follow the trinity of wrinkle-free, designer-styled religions: connect to your spiritual energy, have an aarti have a bite, feng shui, art of living and reiki: have an aarti have a bite, rediscovered by a japanese christian minister, a melange of jesus and buddha, purified love – the perfume of the day. have an aarti have a bite. aarti is celebrated every evening, at every ghat and in every show. in khabhi kushi khabhi gham kajol sways the lamp in every scene, over-pitching values and hierarchy. aarti as light food, as airport art. aarti as the vital symbol of the hindutva forces, who have established themselves as lobbyists for the cloned gods, but who do not care about the living sacred. they do not clean ganga mataji (on the contrary: all the keepers and carers i met were all open-minded, humane and anti-ideological people). but they protect the holy name of varanasi by preventing deepa mehtas film "water". holiness is an image without a core, it is an axiom. it is the godfather of all cloned gods. It is celebrated through aarti.

a day's trip upriver from the sangam lies kanpur. industrial kanpur, heavy duty, tannery muck flowing into the ganga. for a footfull of guchi. how does a visionary see kanpur? After all, he has founded an association – resurgent kanpur it is called. The business card is elegant. his plan is to attract call centres to kanpur. the daughter of the visionary works in a call centre near delhi. The visionaries of kanpur are impressed by what they hear. 1200 jobs, 1200 indians sitting one next to the other in one large room, all of them staring onto computer screens which transport them across oceans into another corporate net, the net of general electrics. they are on the phone, all day long, they consult the screen while they talk with a customer from a suburb in atlanta who wants his appliance serviced. cash or contract? the cash payer receives preferential treatment. he is given the next free slot, the information is typed into the computer, processed by the software, the technician is automatically informed. thank you very much for calling and have a nice day. indian voices conversing about the weather in the usa (hurricane in florida?, montana snowed in?), small-talking about major political, social issues. thank you very much for calling and have a nice day. indian ears understanding every accent. schooled in intensiv courses, in a call centre college, like the one resurgent kanpur wants to set up. the students watch soap operas, serials. they need to demusicalise their speech. thank you very much for calling and have a nice day. bland pronounciation is required. and should the customer inquire: you are not american, are you,? they shall answer with a non-commited "yes". only if further pressured, shall they acknowledge their indian identity. after work they can go home and celebrate aarti, as if nothing has happened. kabhi khushi kabhi gham.

kumbha mela 2001. every morning we wake up to the screech of 108 godly names, our alarm clock is a suffocating mist of song and sound, a dawn full of clanking crickets. Incantations, each prayer besieged by a multitude of competing prayers. no holiness, no solidarity, no inwardness, no mercy. only noise. and the loudest of all mantras, the ultimate destroyer of sleep - "shanti ohm".

one of the most successful american entrepreneurs of indian origin is a man called bose. his company produces loudspeakers – he holds a commanding presence at the kumbh mela. bose is a true globalist, a believer in discontinuity, for he enforces every message, every point of view, every shloka. bose enables the soundtrack for the aarti to resonate along the river banks, to flood the ghats. the sound cosmos is constantly changing: levels rising, volumes dropping, speakers faltering. this is a cultural reality of modern india, this seemingly chaotic installation, this synchronicity, every moment identity is made and unmade. dentities are exchanged, distinctions erased. the poet, the archivist, the commentator may wish to find words for ganga's flow. no sooner have their words found form, they are outdated by a changed river, by the swirl and whirl, they need to make another effort, which will instantaneously be flushed away by a new reality, which they may want to describe and evaluate. They need to change thir language, they start using ulatbamsi – but upside-down is also two-dimensional.

when mtv was introduced to india, the people in charge thought that pop music is like cocacola – you only need to distribute the plastic cups to be successful. the international program was screened in india, the local office was told to focus on marketing. mtv enjoy. but the young indians didn't enjoy it. they found the program uncouth and impolite. the music was too heavy and too black. too much grunge from pearl jam, too much rap from puff daddy. mtv was cornered in a niche of the market. the customer had passed judgement. mtv reacted quickly and boldly. the channel was draped in the indian tricolore, 90% of the videos shown were indian, the vj were told too get rid of the english accent they cultivated so industriously and to get some bambaya masala into their speech. chai boys started advertising for mtv, accompanied by the good old hit: ye jawani, hai diwani. but the mantra remained: mtv enjoy. and on february 14 the program is dedicated to valentine's day. and condom ads are shown, warning of aids. and madhu, a peon in an office, a neo-buddhist, buys his mtv-enjoying wife some flowers. and the good indian music is composed and played on synthesisers, and the musicians can't get enough volume on the monitors and the loudspeakers. so while we are swaying the aarti let us mutter: ohm mtv-enjoy ohm. 108 and 1001 times. but let's delegate this task. let's have a software take care of it, or a robot. let our computers seek darshan on the internet, there are enough cyber mandirs and cloned gods to choose from.

BOMBAY
Advaita on the Suburban

swallow your pride
an elbow in point
choke on the last
morsel of comfort

there is no doubt
we all are one
shedding our skins
to reach the exit

pick up the odour
like a callus a cold
strain with the flow
catching a whiff of border

when the jostling starts
grab the waist
of the nearest prayer
stumble to shanti to amin

body-reading your way
onto the platform
protected by union
from another other.

CAPE TOWN
Ode to Another Whale

Carry me home, stranger,
your rudder is my passport.
When doubts surface
the moon breaks on barren land.

When the surf beats a hasty retreat
The admiral's daughter ties
her hair with tang and hangs
the sailor's laundry on necklaces of pearl.

Draw eyelids on reason, stranger,
give me refuge in your tear.
Where skeletons are scattered
the coast crawls out to pray.

BANGKOK
Maitreya

Tell me what will happen.
A line drawn in curves
Turns to benediction,
Seamed with hawkers
On their own salvation franchise.

At the hour of right angles
A ray lights up the one,
Who is always steadfast
And his marble smile flutters
Over the whims of human limestone.

MEKKA
Collateral Damage

Greedy for righteous action
the pilgrims will not be pacified.
For once the Devil stands still –
hit him with pebbles in hand.

The Devil grins all the way to the stoning,
today he will harvest the vain,
he will lap up blood from foreheads,
he will feed on limping pain.

He cannot miss a marksman
who takes generous aim.

HANOI
One notch higher the poet speaks to mandarins
Temple of Literature

It was here
Underneath these beams
That the students surfaced for clarity
A well-worded page away from heaven.

Admitted to glory and concubines
Your name carved in blue
And carried to posterity by turtles
You might choose to forget:

There is but one character
For pain, for despair
And the melting footsteps
Of a retreating army.

PHNOM PENH
Killing Fields

Wan to see killing fields, mista?
I give you cheap, mista!
Dead cheap?
Wise crack no bone.
Play the numerology game.
One million? Must do better.
Study the entrails of a dumb dog.
Two million? Better than that.
Hold your moistened finger against the wind.
Three million? Convene a round table of seers.
Silence one better than shame.
Ok, let's ride to the skulls.

In a school they gambled with the devil.
Another victory at hand,
he stood up, derision on his tongue:
You always let me win,
me, the most feeble of your excuses.

Afterwards, floating to the moon,
a voice of reason blew a fuse.
Wan to have lady massage, mista?
I give you cheap, mista!
Not as cheap as skulls, though.

JAIPUR
The Sun Dial of Sawai Jai Singh

At his birth
the court astrologers sketched
a future for the future king.
Simple means are most exact.

Jai Singh, king at eleven,
became an astronomer.
A mathematician.
He read Ptolemy,
he read Euclid,
he read Isaac Newton
and Mohammed Ulug Beg.

He decided to measure the sun
more exactly than ever before.

The first shadows took steps of twenty seconds.
That was not good enough for Jai Singh.
He built a stairway to the stars,
that only ended,
when his kingdom ran out of marble.
Through the day the sun melted by seconds;
at night, cross-legged on the top-most step,
he pointed his watchful eye
towards the many lights thrown back at him.

This clock has fallen behind by eleven minutes,
says the woman from under her broad brim,
and stretches her pale arm out to Jai Singh.
Madam, the sun is never wrong.
The time is right for this spot,
where we stand together.
The watch that you wear
is correct wherever you go
but not here.

DUBAI
GUESTS CHECKED-IN AT THE DUBAI HOTEL AND HOTEL APARTMENTS IN 2004: 5,420,724
2003: 4,980,228
AVERAGE LENGTH OF STAY: 2.80 DAYS.
HOTEL INDUSTRY'S TOTAL REVENUES 2004: 6,205,748,480
OCCUPANCY: 76.9 % BEDS

THE DEPARTMENT HAS BEEN ENGAGED IN AGGRESSIVE MARKETING AND
PROMOTIONAL CAMPAIGN TO ACHIEVE THE GOAL OF ATTRACTING 15 MILLION
TOURISTS BY THE YEAR 2010.

SRW

028

ห้าม
ปิดป้ายโฆษณา

กรุณาใส่กุญแจประตูตู้ข่านเมื่อตรวจสอบคู่สายเสร็จ
กุญแจตู้ผ่าน ชำรุด-สูญหาย-เปิดตู้ไม่ได้
ติดต่อ รกตต.1.1(2) ทร5.0-2259-7142,0-2251-7136-38

DE
THE
A
TH
UATA
CINDY
HOBIT
FOR
327F

PRISONERS *PER 1000 INHABITANTS*
RUANDA: 15.34
BURKINA FASO: 0.21

TELEPHONE LINES *PER 1000 INHABITANTS*
MONACO: 1,043.34
DEMOCRATIC REPUBLIC OF THE CONGO: 0.38

MOBILE PHONES *PER 1000 INHABITANTS*
UNITED ARAB EMIRATES: 1,177.61

CARS PER 1000 INHABITANTS
1 SAN MARINO: 926.32
2 ANDORRA: 892.70
3 JERSEY: 795.58
4 LIECHTENSTEIN: 718.56
5 MONACO: 712.07
6 LUXEMBOURG: 661.34
7 NEW ZEALAND: 633.47
8 ISLE OF MAN: 619.81
9 ARUBA: 618.51
10 GUERNSEY: 599.08

TELEVISION SETS PER 1000 INHABITANTS
1 FAROE ISLANDS: 1,040.69
2 BERMUDA: 1,015.38
3 GREAT BRITAIN: 978.42
4 SWEDEN: 970.07
5 UNITED STATES OF AMERICA: 937.07
6 LATVIA: 893.17
7 NORWEGEN: 887.51
8 DENMARK: 886.69
9 CAYMAN ISLANDS: 858.47
10 MONACO: 835.91

PIGS *PER 1000 INHABITANTS*
1 DENMARK: 2,046
2 TUVALU: 1,200
3 SAMOA: 1,103
4 TONGA: 780
5 NETHERLANDS: 756
10 UNITED ARAB EMIRATES: 0

FISH (KG) *PER 1000 INHABITANTS*
1 FAROE ISLANDS: 11,391.90
37 UNITED ARAB EMIRATES: 46.75

SHEEP *PER 1000 INHABITANTS*
1 NEW ZEALAND: 11,217
64 UNITED ARAB EMIRATES: 210

POULTRY *PER 1000 INHABITANTS*
1 BRUNEI: 36,682
11 UNITED ARAB EMIRATES: 8,994

E

105 VICTI
25 KILE
67 LOST

DOCTORS PER 1000 INHABITANTS
1 ITALY: 6.15
2 CUBA: 5.93
3 USA: 5.49
4 MONACO: 4.95
5 BELARUS: 4.50
6 GREECE: 4.41
7 BELGIUM: 4.23
8 RUSSIA: 4.23
9 SAN MARINO: 4.21
10 LITHUANIA: 4.07
59 EGYPT: 2.12

Santa Mo

Santa Monica

SEX INDUSTRY

WORLDWIDE PORN SALES 57 BILLION $. (MICROSOFT 36.8 BILLION $)

60% OF ALL WEBSITE VISITS ARE SEXUAL IN NATURE

THE NUMBER 1 SEARCH TERM USED AT SEARCH ENGINE SITES IS THE WORD SEX

HOLLYWOOD CURRENTLY RELEASES 11,000 ADULT MOVIES PER YEAR, MORE THAN 20 TIMES THE MAINSTREAM MOVIE PRODUCTION

AMERICANS RENT UPWARDS OF 800 MILLION PORN VIDEOS AND DVD'S A YEAR (3.6 BILLION NONPORN VIDEOS)

THE PORN INDUSTRY EMPLOYS AN EXCESS OF 12,000 PEOPLE IN CALIFORNIA

IN CALIFORNIA ALONE THE PORN INDUSTRY PAYS OVER $36 MILLION IN TAXES EVERY YEAR

MOST GIRLS WHO ENTER THE PORN INDUSTRY DO ONE VIDEO AND QUIT

THE EXPERIENCE IS SO PAINFUL, HORRIFYING, EMBARRASSING, HUMILIATING FOR THEM THAT THEY NEVER DO IT AGAIN

THE TOTAL REVENUE FROM PROSTITUTION IN THAILAND: 59-60% OF THE GOVERNMENT'S BUDGET FOR ANY GIVEN YEAR

IN NEW ZEALAND: THE MAJORITY OF THE 6,000-8,000 PROSTITUTES ARE ASIAN

IN AUCKLAND: OF THE 4,000 PROSTITUTES 800 ARE THAI, 400 ARE OF OTHER ASIAN ORIGIN

IN JAPAN

OVER 150,000 NON-JAPANESE WOMEN WORK IN PROSTITUTION, MOSTLY THOSE OF THAI AND PHILIPINO DESCENT

JAPANESE MEN CONSTITUTE THE LARGEST NUMBER OF ASIAN SEX TOURISTS

THE SEX INDUSTRY ACCOUNTS FOR 1% OF THE GNP AND IS EQUAL WITH JAPAN'S DEFENSE BUDGET

TOKYO'S SEX ZONE HAS ONLY 0.34 SQ. KM. AND COUNTS WITHIN IT 3,500 SEX FACILITIES; STRIP THEATERS, PEEP SHOWS,

"SOAPLANDS," "LOVERS", "BANKS", PORNO SHOPS, SEX TELEPHONE CLUBS, KARAOKE BARS, CLUBS, ETC.

ica Freeway

an Bernardino

K HER

R HER NUMBER

IS BORING

YOUR WIFE

LLION WAYS TO MEET
DY. COULD YOU IMAGINE?
ARD TO START AND GET 20.000 $

73

A HUNDR

'NSURAN

YEARS

ONE-PARTY AND NO-PARTY STATES
PEOPLE'S REPUBLIC OF CHINA (COMMUNIST PARTY OF CHINA)
CUBA (COMMUNIST PARTY OF CUBA)
ERITREA (PEOPLE'S FRONT FOR DEMOCRACY AND JUSTICE)
DEMOCRATIC PEOPLE'S REPUBLIC OF KOREA (WORKERS' PARTY OF KOREA)
LAOS (LAO PEOPLE'S REVOLUTIONARY PARTY)
LIBYA (NO-PARTY STATE)
SYRIA (ARAB SOCIALIST BA'TH PARTY)
TURKMENISTAN (DEMOCRATIC PARTY OF TURKMENISTAN)
VIETNAM (COMMUNIST PARTY OF VIETNAM)

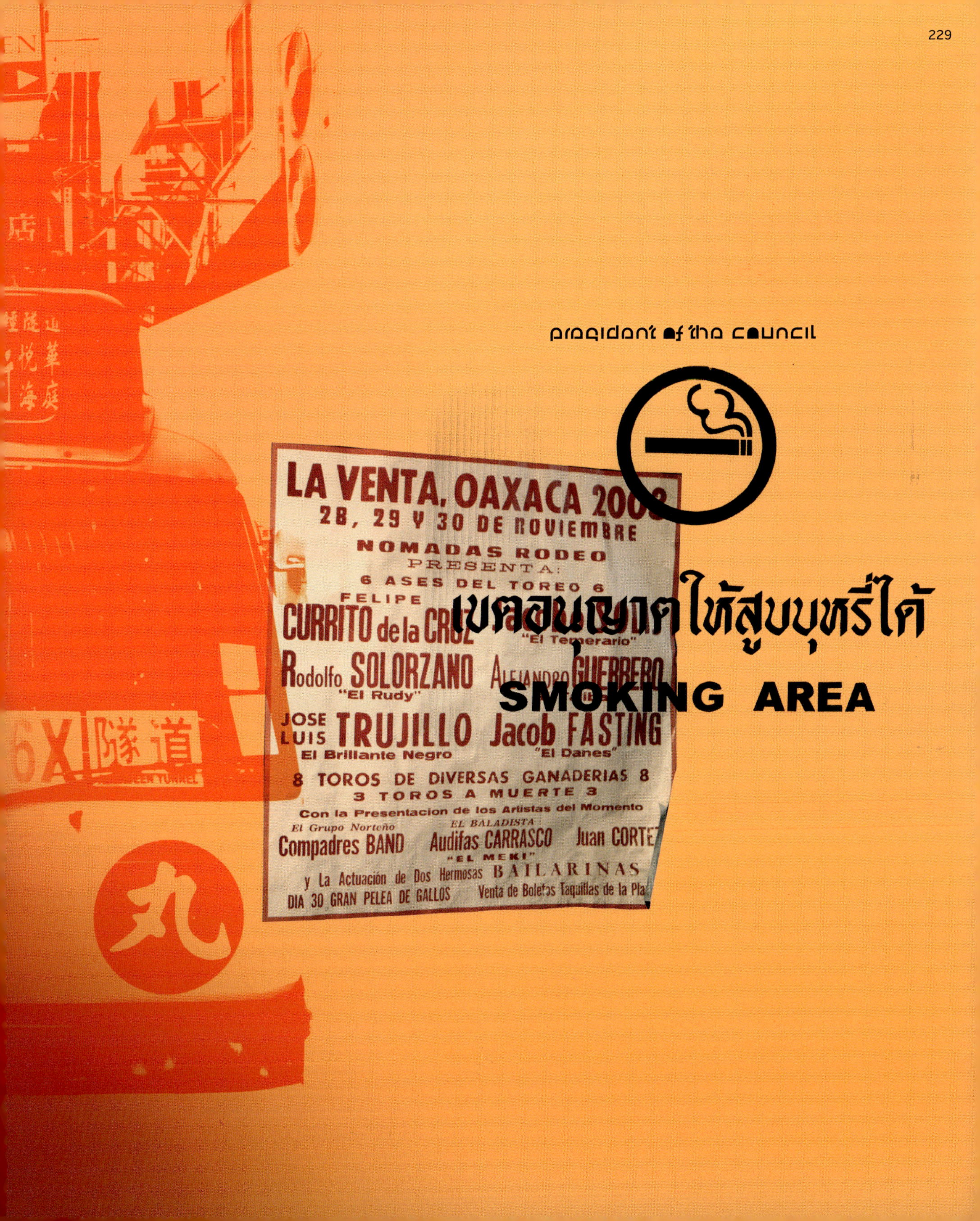

president of the council

เขตอนุญาตให้สูบบุหรี่ได้

SMOKING AREA

LVMH GROUP, *MOËT HENNESSY LOUIS VUITTON*, MOËT & CHANDON, DOM PÉRIGNON, VEUVE CLICQUOT, KRUG, MERCIER, RUINART, CHÂTEAU D'YQUEM, CHANDON ESTATES, HENNESSY, CLOUDY BAY, CAPE MENTELLE, NEWTON, MOUNT ADAM, LOUIS VUITTON, CÉLINE, LOEWE, BERLUTI, KENZO, GIVENCHY, CHRISTIAN LACROIX, MARC JACOBS, FENDI, STEFANOBI, EMILIO PUCCI, THOMAS PINK, DONNA KARAN, ELUXURY, TAG HEUER, ZENITH, CHRISTIAN DIOR MONTRES, FRED, CHAUMET, OMAS, GUERLAIN, PARFUMS CHRISTIAN DIOR, PARFUMS GIVENCHY, KENZO PERFUMES, LAFLACHÈRE, BENEFIT COSMETICS, FRESH, MAKE UP FOR EVER, ACQUA DI PARMA, PERFUMES LOEWE, DFS, MIAMI CRUISELINE SERVICES, SEPHORA, LE BON MARCHÉ, LA SAMARITAINE

LOTUS COLLECTION
LATEST EUROPEAN FASHION
NEWLY CREATED HEAVY FANC
FASHION FABRIC FOR THE YEAR
HIPPER ONE TONE DYED
"HIPPER ONE TONE DYED"
58" X   2 5   YDS
M.I.C.

BRAND VALUE *IN $ MILLIONS/COUNTRY*
1 COCA-COLA: 67.525 / USA
2 MICROSOFT : 59.941 / USA
3 IBM: 53.376 / USA
4 GE 46.996 / USA
5 INTEL 35.588 / USA
6 NOKIA 26.452 / FINLAND
7 DISNEY 26.441 / USA
8 MCDONALD'S 26.014 / USA
9 TOYOTA 24.837 / JAPAN
10 MARLBORO 21.189 / USA
11 MERCEDES-BENZ 20.006 / GERMANY
12 CITI 19.967 / USA
13 HEWLETT-PACKARD 18.866 / USA
14 AMERICAN EXPRESS 18.559 / USA
15 GILLETTE 17.534 / USA

DAILY CONSUMPTION *(CAL) PER CAPITA*
1 AUSTRIA: 3,820
2 USA: 3,790
3 GREECE: 3,770
4 PORTUGAL: 3,770
5 BELGIUM: 3,710
6 IRELAND: 3,690
7 ITALY: 3,690
8 SAN MARINO: 3,690
9 FRANCE: 3,680
10 LIECHTENSTEIN: 3,620
207 ERITREA: 1,670
208 BURUNDI: 1,640
209 SOMALIA: 1,640
210 CONGO: 1,560

10 ³⁰ am.

12 pm.

ATTE.

Casa de
Gaby

GROSS DOMESTIC PRODUCT *IN US$*

EUROPEAN UNION: 12,623,113

1 UNITED STATES: 11,667,515
2 JAPAN: 4,623,398
3 GERMANY: 2,714,418
4 UNITED KINGDOM: 2,140,898
5 FRANCE: 2,002,582
6 PEOPLE'S REPUBLIC OF CHINA (MAINLAND): 1,932,093
7 ITALY: 1,672,302
8 SPAIN: 991,442
9 CANADA: 979,764
10 INDIA: 691,876
178 SOLOMON ISLANDS: 24
179 MICRONESIA, FED. STS.:
180 TONGA: 213

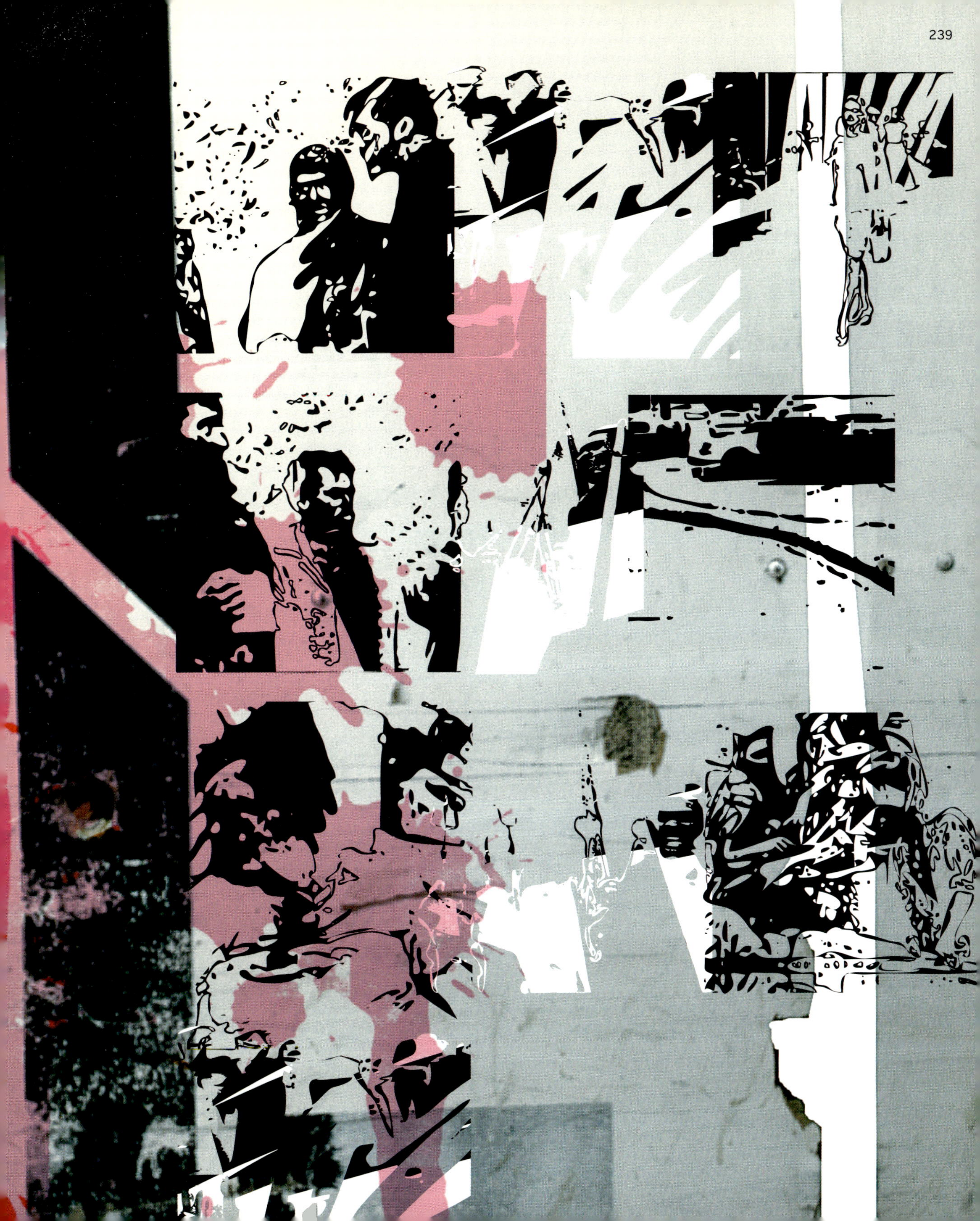

RATE OF DEFORESTATION
BRAZIL: 2,550,000
INDONESIA : 1,080,000

SPECIES PER TEN SQUARE KM OF RAINFOREST
750 SPECIES OF TREES
125 TYPES OF MAMMAL
400 VARIETIES OF BIRDS
100 DIFFERENT KINDS OF REPTILES
60 AMPHIBIANS
AN AVERAGE TREE MAY BE THE HOME TO OVER 400 DIFFERENT INSECT SPECIES

ICE CREAM CONSUMPTION *IN LITERS PER CAPITA*
1 NEW ZEALAND: 26.3
2 USA: 18.7
3 AUSTRALIA: 17.8
4 FINLAND: 13.9
5 SWEDEN: 11.9
6 CANADA: 9.5
7 ITALY: 9.2
8 IRELAND: 9.0
9 DENMARK: 8.7
10 GREAT BRITAIN: 7.7
11 CHILE: 5.6
12 MALAYSIA: 2.0
13 CHINA: 1.9
14 JAPAN: 0.01

HE-MOON AND SHE-MOON

GEDICHTE

JOSÉ F.A. OLIVER

To write and eying words, to eye them, like the trackers raise the hidden hunt and to be the hunted, pursued relentlessly by letter-accomplices. Pace of words without repose, track of prints, pasturing of rest: To exist of words so as to be inside them. Shy and tender. Tender and calm like fingertips that caress strange skin. Today, which is already tomorrow, I am searching for my tongues.

Mondzunge, lengua luna, moon-tongue. Those day-falls of pale lights and shades, which became familiar nights and moons, pale lightrivering of the sky, remain close to me. There was a house of two houses. Two houses like two cultures. A house with two floors and a lullaby of nonwords melted the rhythm of uncertainties and two languages. Open doors and windows into forgotten voyages. The Alemannic dialect of the first floor, the Andalusian of the second. In-between steps without gender and the beginning of a game. Draft of the gender game. The bodies of the words, their souls. Only a few steps separating she-moon and he-moon, *la luna, der Mond.*

To submerge myself. Simply to dive into that current of fathers and ancestors, of mothers, at last. Breath and omen. Evidently I remain, evidently audible. To wander near the discarded, the farthest separated. To breathe between the rags of tongues and perhaps to challenge those language guards and alpha-beasts that incite me to name. I, to exist of earthen words, yearn for my languages like the host for the good friend.

My lives, so peculiarly mine, respond continuously to these nights of antecedents, sudden dawns, days of pure invention. Set pieces like tongues of earth. Biographies and remote histories resembling theatre. Monologues of satiated pleasures. Keeping me company, the worn-out wings of an interrupted play that debuts unceasingly, and, like every uninvited guest, these lives arrive to upset my world of attitudes and contradictions. Intruders on my stage of roving theatrics. Hunters of shores. Timid underground lovers like blood brothers.

Memories of a childhood in the Black Forest. Images of the time etched in the mind, summers at dusk and pitchforks of hay. Playing *Fongis,* after homework, jumping on haystacks at nightfall with the children on my street. The bells and their ring of prayer and the admonitions of the adults always within earshot. The continuous reprimands following and falling into bed, beaten to a pulp. The gaiety anticipated by the next reveille. The first rays of sun and fresh cut grass. The whistles of the scythes. Green-wets. The flavour of sap. Like that, day smelled of day. Like that, childhood smelled of summers in short sleeves.

Days like children. Days on light soles, where the moss, the juice of the red currants and the quince trees seduced me to forgetting. I discovered how to dream and they let me. Without truly becoming conscious, in my little-great universe, of what was dream and what would cease being one. In summer I dreamed just as I was afraid in autumn, hiding myself from those monstrous light-swallowing clouds, hurling kites at them to make myself master of peril: Young Master of Tempests before a grey canvas. But all the daring, in the end, only to bring me closer to my fears and distresses, surreptitiously to my mother's skirt while she hung out the clothes. The wind spelling our attachment and the storm saying nothing less than protection.

The winters were of snow. Masses of snow. I haven't stopped caressing those afternoons, closed in by its white coat. I remember descending in sleighs, the Chasms of Death and the oranges in my mittens. Smell of the south beyond the ice chute like the wakeful nights on each trip back to the little homeland bearing toward Andalusia. I remember the slices of bread with jam, confections of cherry or strawberry, laid on thick, and that ancient little heat of our glazed tile stove that let us thaw after quixotic descents through sleigh courses that we had traced ourselves, plunging downhill: "Look out below! Sausage and mashed potatoes!" – Instants of a childhood in which I was one more among them. An expert in the games of the occasion.

Still, there was someone that escaped slyly from those hidden idylls merely through his undeniable presence. Serenely surprised, and, at times, wounded. Someone who, essentially, was not of the native soil. At least, he couldn't go unnoticed at *vesper-meals* of pure smoked *Speck*, dinner well earned after the production-line haying that brought unity and solidarity to the neighbours, who showed a disposition for mutual help never seen before, facing the August storms that loomed maliciously; or someone who didn't fit into the wintry landscapes with its pork-fat sandwiches, the pointed hats and the red, frozen noses. That "Someone", no one but this One, had constructed with the lies of the time a refuge from questions and yearnings.

I had dug myself a den and I furnished it. A hospitable hideout in case the Other, which was confined in me, threatened to escape. The one that had to model a little sailor suit every Sunday afternoon, totally incomprehensible to the first, and white to top it off. Almost ready, so gallantly presented, he regarded the sight of himself with an air of embarrassment: decorated in that blue of extreme sea, that sailor-white, and covered in little gold buttons besides; becoming excessively angry, or as angry as the moment required, then suddenly, standing up straight as a stick, because he would have done anything to escape to the forest that bordered his house to play cops and robbers. Despite every resistance, Sunday went as Sundays must. Out of habit and faithful fulfilment of the tradition that was destroying the world, he was condemned to a pilgrimage with some twenty adults – though the exact number of participants is secondary – and, with his showy, southern appearance and purely immigrated stock, he played his part, grumbling or no, in the Sunday Andalusian rally of the promenading Spanish educators and their respective pupils. Vacant footbridge over rocky paths for little decorative puppets. Custom and its cultivation à la Andalusian before the amazed eyes of the Alemannic hunting village scenes. What else could he have done, the poor thing. Through experience, he knew pretty well the traitor the little Black Forest grass stain could be, ornamenting any little white suit that roved outside of its clear destination, though when he looked carefully, it seemed the light green on white background could very subtly outline the colours of the Andalusian flag.

Even then, it was impossible to avoid the impression that Sundays were pulling us gaudily toward the typical, which is to say, for the Germans, much more manifestly *ehpanisch* than during the week – and I use this Andalemannic word with no desire to delve into what today signifies the abstruse and unfortunate concept "to be German or to be Spanish". Be that as it may, on the days of the Lord, the gathering – southern, heaped by dozens with their Muslim reminiscences and Hebrew preclamors – seemed to unburden itself, and it seemed it would always be so, when the Andalusian Spaniards of that little Black Forest village – whose name out of discretion I don't want to mention at this point – would meet each other to breathe their own air on walks with such strict speed limits, they threatened to break the record for slowness (for which they can be counted as precursors to urban speed restrictions). Imagine: an hour or more sometimes for a stretch of a hundred meters; just to take a little air and dream of eggplants; figs; red, ripe tomatoes; to dissolve along those passionate Iberian strolls the milestones lost, like the world, between Andalusia and that Black Forest hamlet (whose name out of respect I continue guarding in secret), which is to say, erasing the distance between their daily lives and their yearning for the south. Kilometer after kilometer yielded and returned home. North-less.

Always at their side, we children. Full of carefully staged duties that we couldn't stand. Remote voices from a lacquer recording like a skipping record of ritualised niceties. Affectionatly pampered. Well prepared. They offered us sandwiches of chocolate with bananas. Sugar-water for thirst, under lovpressive kisses, caresses and fingers raised among a disturbance of hands, that gesticulated without order or concert, that more than once flew out, missed and corrected themselves quickly – delivering us exquisite ear-plums straight from the fatherland. A food-beating – not only for the first-born, whom they served dessert twice as tart-torture – which we took bitterly and felt like another tenderness from the paternal palate of the mother tongue, and yet received with no uncertain pride. They couldn't humilate us. Ever. The little sailor suit demanded posture. A posture of dignity.

Always at their side, we children. Sundayed, dressed and loved. We walked snivelling our heads off and carrying them more haughtily through our Alemannic Ramblas, as complete marvels passed before our eyes: stalls full of flowers, merchants selling birds, taverns, snacks and drinks, fiestas, donkeys and blind alleys. All along our Stations of the Cross we brushed the edges of a plaza, one that began to fill itself with friends, relatives, and uncountable dead as we turned and turned through the enigmatic Avenue of Memory. A Plaza Mayor whose funny stories, coincidences and passing tragedies made the old ones cry, pulled the adults into thought, and made the kids laugh. That was the chaotic struggle of San Quintin – hell in the making. (I had no idea then who that man and saint was, Saint Idon'tknowho...). All right then.

In those places there wasn't anyone to hinder them, no one that could throw them out. Not them or their children.

I believe that we, the educatees, must have left a strange impression in the eyes of the natives as we picked up the step with obedient indifference, and, served on a silver platter, we must have presented a few fine examples, singular really, the best gems the Culture of Spanish Emigration could exhibit in those days.

Lightly indignant and stupefied at once, in the days of divine repose we moved in another caravan. Behind us dreams, ahead, phantasmagoria. Confined by languages, desires, memories, silences, recipes, and complaints, we saw ourselves suddenly pulled into the illusions and tears of the adults who we examined during the week in equally surprising incidents, when they entered or left their shifts: a savory and copious selection on the imaginary table; exotic morsels of memory like sweets, and little porcelain figurines – those daily glories completely wasted – but who on Sundays, in all their splendor, made us little and tiny little Spaniards. Time meaning nothing when the factory time-stamper stopped.

So they adorned me and exterminated me very Spanishly. They washed, groomed and perfumed me. "Heno de Pravia" they called that damned fragrance. I don't know how many leagues it travelled on the wind. I penetrated through people and landscapes, leaving an odorless substance that brought on the ancestors, the reason we carried liters of that contraband cologne, always when we crossed the French-German border at Kehl, on our way back from Spain. Sundays I understood why. The working days, without a doubt, I couldn't help seeing myself changed into a chubby-cheeked Black Forest rascal who looked well fed, local and robust in *Lederhosen*, those short little trousers made of deer-skin, which were never to be washed, and which, apart from covering and revealing certain parts, served to clean the fat off the knives they used to cut the *Speck*. And not only in August.

There I saw myself again: untied and tied at once, before another distinct language that smelled of earth, which made forget the dead and which, though I would realize it much later, would reject us. Which had to reject us. German without being German. Spanish without being Spanish. In movement: I. And, among my "*Is*", consciousness.

A master of the rules of the games of the place that little by little were being seen outside of the game, just as he kept entering, dominating the rules in order to break them.

My little lair, my peculiar hideout, in those days, was under a balcony, a kind of wooden veranda, already aging and raised on stilts, that served as a lookout. My place. Behind heaps of kindling, stacked against the cold of winter:

A desk I had constructed of a few swiped fruit boxes, and paper – the tatters of paid invoices and snippets of bills that I had saved from certain death in the bonfire – and pencils. We were intimate friends. Accomplices.

Both searching for a tongue.

I and the Other.

He-moon and she-moon. *Lunesa Luna Mondin. Mond.*

UNTERSCHLUPF IN BERN
[der versuch 1 müllbehälter zu beschriften]

die englische vokabel : to emerge 1 TINTENWISCH / leb
loses tier in schlieren [verwesungsmetastasen]. Was übrig

staut im müllbehälter 1 totentanz / vokabeltest
to emerge = w:ort : „where the war

begins". KEHRICHT
GESTAMMEL unterhäuft

fleischkugeln brot nüsslersalat & broccoli
1 schwamm die wörterbalz gebläht / zerfall

im werden aktualitäten & aufgestopft
den deckelplastikbecher /

1 milchkaffee
der war / & 1 wasserglas [almosenlang]

pluraltrocken zeichnen lippen auf
kippen beleg um bilderstummel 1 schmecken nach

& weitere notate / schreibkonsum
: 1 satz begehren vor dem blick /

filterskulptur & bröselaug
zerknülltes altpapier danach ist

zustandsstill 1 schwarz
& unbeleuchtet nachts geruchsgerangel

1 bleistiftkopf in fleck & zeichen
die schrift & aufgerissen

„where the war begins". Könnte
von orientierung sein

wo 1 datum klebt an speise
eis & herzverlangen & to emerge

where the war begins & all
die namen

geworfen
1 schattenreif der wörter 1 zeitungsschliff

: 1 notlust voll
& einvergesssen weltgefüttert

das scherbenohr ganz gitter halt /
betongelecktes schauen & graues fleisch

ganz nachtvergessen ganz blindes aug
& federleicht

wenn's nacht wird. Ganz

(für Hans Ruprecht)

CHIRURGISCHES GEDICHT.1 EINGRIFF 1 WEITERLEBEN

im zehnten jahr die traueranzeige erneut
in der hand [september 1995]. Vater
sagte „ich will ein blumen
loses grab". Mutter sagte
will nicht an seinem todestag
will nicht den todestag
die todesnacht
herausschneiden
die trauer. Den HERZGERUCH
setzen heuer rosmarin olivenblatt &
1 SCHWEIGGEDICHT [„marmorschweigen"]. Jedes
bildgedächtnis ist 1 bildbrand 1 nachtoleander
ins herzgerippe eingewachsen
1 HERZVERNARBEN

: BEOBACHTE

1 *mädchen mit roten schuhen*
& entengeräusche 1 entenzunge
obsidiangrüne augen. Beobachte
den landschritt *geht an land /*
wird von der mutter aus dem rad-
anhänger gehievt / geht vierbeinig geht
mit 1 mutterstütze. Beobachte
in die schritte eingewoben / verschnürt
atemzöpfe 1 schwere zartheit
1 augenfroh
1 engelsgestalt der haare. Über allem
1 lebensgegend

ZWISCHENBERICHTE. 1 ZEITGEDICHT

050804

die zeitung von gestern
im wurmstich 1 apfel
versteck & pupille der katze

den schleichweg gegangen
die grenze missachtet. Die augen
hinter den pässen verborgen

1 mundecho
sprechbündel
schreibohr

im zöllner 1 datum
1 stempelverschwimmen
& regung von angst. Domestiziert

so foltern die staaten erklären
so foltern die briten erklären
so foltern die foltern erklären

die zeitung von heute
im angebot wörter
kaschemmen auf see

gestrandetes wasser
1 alp auf der zunge
die leibesvisiten

aus trunkenen häusern
verknotete spiele
aus anschlag & anschlag

& fußballberichte
börsianertabellen
die zeitung von morgen

1 kochrezept neugier
1 kochrezept trauma
: die wörter verenden

United States Postal Service
Customs Declaration and Dispatch Note — CP 72
Sender's Name
Business
Street
City
Country
From
To
NO stop any TIME
Certificate Number(s) (13)
Date and sender's signature (15)
PS Form 2976-A, January 2004

STEP
UP
AND
down

NO STOPPING
ANYTIME
United States Postal Service
Customs Declaration and Dispatch Note — CP 72
Do not duplicate this form without USPS approval.
2ACPRI-04-P-6014
1 - Customs Declaration
PS Form 2976-A, January 2004
DIFC | Dubai International Financial Centre
CP096841322US

YESTERDAY ALL MY TROUBLE!

PENCIL AND PAPER
A WRITER NEEDS THE RESISTANCE OF THE BLANK PAGE

BLEISTIFT UND PAPIER
DER SCHRIFTSTELLER BRAUCHT DEN WIDERSTAND DES LEEREN BLATTES

LÁSZLÓ CSIBA

No one knows what we humans are. Self-control, for instance, is scientifically irrelevant. Self-knowledge does not give proof of any particular achievement. Another well-known fact: despair cannot be solved using mathematics. So, what are human beings? We do not know. We can merely learn about their thoughts and deeds, or watch them grow old.

We have nothing to reproach ourselves with. We do not make things easy for ourselves. We can be thankful, but not praise ourselves. We can only praise that which has made us what we are today.

We know this: there is not success, but there are plans. The pencil is filled to the brim with awakenings and moments of pause, with intuition and becoming, with silence and screams, with ashes and time. Fact is: I want to write, I want to find words within myself, in order to learn who I am and what I think.

Writing is, as we all know, a hard and poorly-paid profession. Then, why write?

Now and again, we go shopping and return home with a sudden idea, one that knows no compromise. One that excites us, challenges us. An idea that can last an entire day, and the writer can write, the narrator can narrate, keeping a clear head, saving the body from sinking into a high bog land of futility. I am the pencil that gets used up with every word. I am the paper that disappears beneath the words.

Franz Kafka once said, "You need not leave your room. Remain sitting at your table and listen. You need not even listen, simply wait, just learn to become quiet, and still, and solitary. The world will freely offer itself to you ... It has no choice; it will roll in ecstasy at your feet."

I did not come to Germany as a bargain hunter, but as a migrating bird. And soon, I began building a nest. Now, every time I begin to speak in German, I change the identity of my voice. If I had stayed in Hungary, I would have had a language. But I did not stay in Hungary. And so I must make a language. For me, being here means being language. Somewhere in my body Hungary lives on intact. Is there a purpose, a meaning that lies beneath all that comes to pass? In the spring when the birds scream, we understand. But their silence in winter is a mystery to us. The fact is this: I am alive. The question is this: how can I use this opportunity?

I was born into a village and became a villager. I grew up in a small town and became a provincial. I came to adulthood in a big city and became a metropolitan. I frequently fled from the big city into nature and during the last three decades I have become a lover and child of nature. In nature I have learned how to walk: what I mean by this is that I have learned how to walk a path that no one before me has walked, my own path. And all I saw and discovered, I could call by its name. I walked through a dense wood of words and in time I became a wordsmith.

I only have German words now: they torment, taunt and exalt me. I must deal with them to find the meaning of my life. I must employ a language that I do not have complete command of.

This makes me very weary, but is a fact which is not obvious. The process of finding a balance between my language fatigue and my language efforts releases an energy inside of me that sometimes hinders failure.

And I am able, I am allowed to continue, to keep on trying to convince those German words that I exist, so that the German language will accept and adopt me. When I spend day after day looking for a way out, I must look for or invent myself. When I look for myself I look for the first sentence, with all its endings and new beginnings, with all its losses and small successes. My presence here has gradually turned into an idea of Germany, into a great slow thought, which I have not abandoned till this very day.

> the german word
> is my today,
> the falling stone
> the chair,
> the desk,
> the bed,
> one two steps,
> the unbroken gait ...
>
> the german word
> describes
> the unknown me,
> the one who remains tethered
> to a post of
> used pencils ...

And we ask ourselves: what do humans need to live? Our daily bread? Clothes? A roof over our heads? Or a dream?

Those who feel, experience adventure. And yet, is happiness really the highest of emotions? Happiness does not mean everything to me. But the goodness in people does. There, where I was a child there now grow elder-bushes. The worn path which ran below the bank slope has become overgrown. The space now offers an open view out over the plain, where every voice has a name. But can we rely on memories?

"Life must be a great privilege if we, in the end, have to pay for it by dying," says Imre Kertész.

I write from within a void to no one. Why do I write? Maybe, to give myself unparalleled diversion and amusement, so that it is easier for me to stand myself. Maybe, to quench my thirst for vitality. Or, rather because I do that which I am?

On paper there is a hiding place. Here, you can scream for help, you can ask nicely, pray, beg. But no one will hear you. Here, bending over the blank page, you can proceed for a long ways, all alone. Because the longest distances, the greatest expanses, are inside of us. Here, you can climb to heights and silently look down at your life.

I watch how the first sentence on the piece of paper burns. There is a human being in the flames. Silent disappearance, and yet, at the same time, the temptation of immense resistance.

Was der Mensch ist, wissen wir nicht. Die Selbstbeherrschung, zum Beispiel, ist wissenschaftlich belanglos. Die Selbsterkenntnis ist kein Beweis für besondere Leistung. Ebenso ist uns die Tatsache vertraut, dass Verzweiflung mathematisch nicht lösbar ist. Also, was ist der Mensch? Wir wissen es nicht. Wir können lediglich sein Denken und sein Tun erfahren oder sein Altern begleiten.

Wir haben uns nichts vorzuwerfen. Wir haben uns nichts geschenkt. Wir können danken, nicht aber uns preisen. Wir können einzig das loben, was uns zu dem gemacht hat, der wir heute sind.

Wir wissen: Es gibt keinen Erfolg. Aber es gibt Pläne. Der Bleistift ist bis zum Rand voll mit Erwachen und Innehalten, mit Ahnen und Werden, mit Schweigen und Schrei, mit Asche und Zeit. Denn schreiben will ich, Worte in mir finden, um zu erfahren, wo ich bin und was ich denke.

Schreiben ist, und das wissen wir, ein harter und schlecht bezahlter Job. Warum dann schreiben?...

Mitunter gehen wir einkaufen und kehren mit einem Einfall heim, der keine Kompromisse kennt. Ein Reiz ist da. Die Herausforderung ist da. Eine Idee, die für den ganzen Tag reicht, und der Schreiber kann schreiben, der Erzähler erzählen, der Kopf bleibt oben und der Körper geht nicht unter im Hochmoor der Vergeblichkeit. Ich bin der Bleistift, der sich mit jedem Wort abnutzt. Ich bin das Papier, das hinter den Wörtern verschwindet.

„Es ist (wie Franz Kafka meint) nicht notwendig, daß du aus dem Haus gehst. Bleib bei deinem Tisch und horche. Horche nicht einmal, warte nur. Warte nicht einmal, sei völlig still und allein. Anbieten wird sich dir die Welt ..., sie kann nichts anderes, verzückt wird sie sich vor dir winden."

Ich kam wie ein Zugvogel und nicht als Schnäppchenjäger nach Deutschland. Bald begann ich, mir ein Nest zu bauen. Wenn ich auf Deutsch zu sprechen anfange, wechsele ich stets die Identität meiner Stimme. Wäre ich in Ungarn geblieben, hätte ich eine Sprache gehabt. Aber ich bin nicht in Ungarn geblieben. So mache ich die Sprache selbst. Hier zu sein, heißt für mich Sprache sein. Während das Land Ungarn irgendwo in meinem Körper unbehelligt weiterlebt. Liegt hinter dem, was geschieht, ein Wille oder eine Bedeutung? Wenn die Vögel im Frühling schreien, verstehen wir. Aber ihr Schweigen im Winter bleibt uns rätselhaft. Der Fakt ist: Ich lebe. Die Frage ist: Was mache ich aus dieser Möglichkeit?

Ich bin in ein Dorf hinein geboren und wurde ein Dorfmensch. Ich bin in einer Kleinstadt aufgewachsen und wurde ein Kleinstadtmensch. Ich bin in einer Großstadt erwachsen geworden und wurde ein Großstadtmensch. Ich ergriff regelmäßig die Flucht aus der Großstadt in die Natur und wurde in den letzten drei Jahrzehnten ein Naturmensch. Ich habe in der Natur gehen gelernt, das heißt, das Gehen auf einem Weg, den noch niemand gegangen ist, meinem eigenen Weg. Was ich da sah und entdeckte, konnte ich benennen. Ich ging jedes Mal durch einen dichten Wald der Wörter und wurde schließlich ein Wortmensch.

Nun gibt es nichts anderes für mich als die deutschen Wörter, die mich peinigen, verspotten und beglücken, mit denen ich den Sinn meines Lebens aushandeln muss. Ich muss mich einer Sprache bedienen, die ich nicht ganz beherrsche. Das ermüdet sehr. Aber das fällt nicht auf. Diese Balance zwischen Sprachermüdung und Sprachbemühung setzt Kräfte frei, die manchmal ein Scheitern verhindern. Und ich kann, ich darf weitermachen, um die deutschen Wörter von meinem Vorhandensein zu überzeugen, um mich von der deutschen Sprache annehmen und adoptieren zu lassen. Wenn ich mich Tag für Tag auf die Suche begebe, einen Ausweg zu finden, so muss ich mich selbst suchen oder erfinden. Auf der Suche nach mir selbst bin ich auf der Suche nach dem ersten Satz, mit den vielen Enden und neuen Anfängen, mit so viel Verlieren und kleinen Siegen. In meinem Hiersein hat sich Deutschland mit der Zeit zu einem großen und langsamen Gedanken entwickelt, den ich bis heute nicht aufgehört habe, zu denken.

> das deutsche wort
> ist mein heute,
> der fallende stein,
> der stuhl,
> der tisch,
> das bett,
> ein zwei schritte,
> der ununterbrochene gang ...
>
> das deutsche wort
> ist
> das unbekannte ich,
> die angepflockte bleibe
> am zaun
> abgenützter bleistifte ...

Und wir fragen uns. Was braucht der Mensch zum Leben? Das tägliche Brot? Kleider? Ein Dach über dem Kopf? Oder eine Vision?

Wer empfindet, lebt im Abenteuer. Doch ist Glück wirklich das höchste aller Gefühle? Ich bin auf das Glück nicht angewiesen. Aber auf das Gute im Menschen schon. Dort, wo ich ein Kind war, steht jetzt der Holunder. Die Wegspur der Jahre unter der Uferböschung ist zugewachsen. Der Raum gibt den Blick frei auf die Ebene, wo jede Stimme einen Namen hatte. Aber sind Erinnerungen zuverlässig?

„Das Leben muss doch ein großes Privileg sein, wenn wir es mit dem Tod bezahlen müssen", sagt Imre Kertész.

Ich schreibe im Nichts an niemanden. Warum ich schreibe? Vielleicht um mir eine erstklassige Abwechselung zu bieten und mich so leichter ertragen zu können. Vielleicht um mein Verlangen nach Vitalität zu stillen. Oder eher, weil ich das machen kann, was ich bin?

Auf dem Papier ist ein Versteck. Hier kannst du um Hilfe schreien, hier kannst du bitten, beten oder flehen. Keiner wird dich hören. Hier kannst du, über das leere Blatt gebeugt, sehr weit im Alleinsein gehen. Denn die längsten Entfernungen, die größten Weiten sind in uns. Hier kannst du auf die höchste Stelle hinaufsteigen und stumm auf dein Leben hinabschauen.

Ich schaue zu, wie auf dem Blatt Papier der erste Satz brennt. In den Flammen ist ein Mensch. Ein lautloses Verschwinden, gleichzeitig die Versuchung eines ungeheuren Widerstandes.

Virtual **Religion** Index
Major link collection.

Bad **Religion** - The Official Site
Official site. History, newsletter, tour dates, news, photos, web cam, merchand... d links.

Religion *Gateway* - Academic Info
Internet resources for the study of religion. Includes pages on religious studies ... comparative religion.

Religion *Religions Religious Studies Page*
Gene Thursby's extensive collection of information and links for the study and i... tation of religions. Categories include religious ...

Religion *and Spirituality* in the Yahoo! Directory
Yahoo! reviewed these sites and found them related to Religion and Spirituality ...

World Religions **Religion** Statistics Geography Church Statist...
Adherents.com is a growing collection of church membership and religion adhe... atistics. Over 44000 statistics for over 4300 ... ith groups from all world ...

American **Religion** *Data Archive*
Collection of quantitative survey data on churches and church membership, rel... professionals, and religious groups (individuals, congregations and ...

American Academy of **Religion**
Learned society and professional association for scholars whose object of stu... ligion.

Religion *News Service*
The RNS calls themselves „an authoritative source of news about religion, ethi... ituality and moral issues." They have been reporting for over 50 years ...

Beliefnet: **religion**, spirituality, prayer, God, angels, politics ...
... Info | Site Map | Article Index | Manage Your Newsletter Subscriptions · Beli... irect RSS Feed | Religion & Spirituality News RSS Feed | What is RSS?

Freedom From **Religion** Foundation, Inc.
National organization of freethinkers (atheists, agnostics) in Madison, Wiscons... king to keep state and church separate and to ... about ...

Religion in Japan
Online-Handbuch zu Buddhismus und Shinto, den beiden Hauptreligionen Japa... Geschichte und Gegenwart.

Raelian **Religion**
The RaelCanada site, promoting „The message from extraterrestrials to mank... given to Rael (Claude Vorilhon) on the planet of the Elohim.

Crosswalk.com - **Religion** Today: A look at the people, issues ...
Religion Today Summaries - October 7, 2005 ... Religion Today Summaries. C... lk Weblog Weekly NEW Newsletter! Crosswalk Presents ...

RELIGION *GOD THEOLOGY* JESUS BELIEF SYSTEMS Chris... cience ...
SELECTSMART.com Compare, Comparison, Contrast, Weigh against, Christia... ce Conservative Christian Humanist Liberal Christian Unitarian U...

Religious and Sacred Texts
Urantia Book · Zen Texts · Zoroastrian Texts · davidwiley.com · family | educati... search | vita · writings | religion | interests | standards | we... tes.

Islam website; Resources for the Study of Islam
Islam: Academic resources for the study of Islam, religion, Qur'an, hadith, Sunn... 'ite Islam, Sufism, Islam in the modern world, Muslim ...

Dallas Morning News | News for Dallas, Texas | **Religion**
Add Religion to your favorite RSS reader ... Religion links Alphabetical list of re... denominations, ... Religion section honored as ... on best ...

Promoting religious understanding, tolerance and freedom.
Conflicts, evolution, science & religion evaluating each other ... Understanding ... ion will lead to inter-religious dialogue. ...

Nielsen's Psychology of **Religion** Pages
Information and resources about psychology and religion.

Religion *News Blog*
Current and archived religion news items, articles and web sites about cults, re... sects and alternative religions from an apologetics perspective

---

Hello Friend,
I am Dr. Borr...
former C.E.O...
tive and con...
partnership
the details, ...
tep. /// This...
your ,,Mana...
mail:<drborr...
telephone nu...
further detai...
afford more ...
be concluded
back throug...
I look forwar...
Dr. Borris C...

From: „DR BORRIS OLGA" <drbor...

olga, and I represent M̶ ̶ ̶ ̶ ̶il Khordokovsky th̶
Yukos Oil Company ̶ ̶ ̶ ̶ ̶ ̶ ̶ ̶ns̶ ̶ ̶ I have a very se̶
̶ntial brief from this ̶ ̶ ̶ ̶ ̶ ̶ ̶ ̶ ̶(h)̶ ̶ to ask for ̶
̶ce-profiling funds ̶ ̶ ̶ ̶$49̶ ̶ ̶ Million. I will̶
̶n summary, the ̶ ̶unds are coming ̶ ̶ta Bank M̶
a legiti̶ ̶ ̶te transaction ̶ ̶ ̶ ̶ ̶ ̶ ̶ ̶ ̶ ̶ ̶ ̶aid 10%̶
̶nt Fees̶ ̶ If y̶ ̶ ̶ ̶ ̶ ̶ ̶ ̶ ̶ ̶ ̶ ̶lease write bac̶
̶@london̶ ̶ ̶ ̶ ̶ ̶ ̶ ̶ ̶ ̶ ̶ ̶ ̶ ̶with your confider̶
r,fax number an̶ ̶ ̶ ̶rovide ̶ ̶ ̶ ̶ ̶ress and I will pro̶
̶d instructions. ̶ ̶ ̶ ̶ email a̶ ̶ ̶ ̶his confidential; we ̶
̶ical problems. //̶ ̶ ̶ ̶ ̶ ̶ ̶ ̶lease note that this n̶
̶in two weeks. P̶ ̶ ̶ ̶ly, p̶ ̶ ̶ck promptly. Writ̶
̶s personal email ̶ ̶ ̶ ̶ writ̶ ̶ ̶ ̶ ̶ ̶ris7@london.net̶
it. /// Regards /̶ ̶ ̶ ̶ ̶ ̶ss <̶ ̶ ̶ ̶ ̶ ̶ ̶ ̶ ̶

̶mon.com> /̶

̶nswer to: drborris7@london ̶

GOOD DAY,
MY NAME IS DELGADO
IRAQ, AS YOU KNOW WE
FUNDS BELONGING TO S
FISCAL CASH .THE tot
DOLLAR BILLS WHICH I
OUR COMMANDANT NOR
to HAVE ANY MONEY I
CAN HELP US IN RECEIV

THIS IS OUR PLAN OF SHARING N
SHIPPING It OUt OF IRAQ,

IRAQ IS A WAR ZONE. WE PLANED ON
YOU ARE INtERESTED I WILL SEND YO

WHEN YOU RECEIVE tHIS LEttER, KINDLY SE
tHE BOI CAN BE SHIPPED OUt IN 48HRS. PLE

RESPECtFULLY,
SGt. DELGADO.

MONEY ?

I AM AN AMERICAN SOLDIER, I SERVE IN THE MILITARY OF THE 1ST ARMORED DIVISION I[...]
[...]BEING ATTACKED BY INSURGENTS EVERYDAY AND CAR BOMBS. WE WHERE LUCKY TO MOVE[...]
[...]HUSSEIN'S FAMILY HOPPING IT WAS A BOMB IN THE BOI, LATER WE FIND OUT IT WAS A[...]
[...]NT IS US$25,000,000 TWENTY FIVE MILLION UNITED STATE DOLLARS IN CASH, MOSTLY 1[...]
[...]IN OUR CO STURDY AT THE MILITARY BASE CAMP, NOW WE FIND IT AS A BIG RISK ON US[...]
[...]QIS PEOPLE GET TO FIND OUT ABOUT THIS BOI OF MONEY BECAUSE WE ARE NOT ALLOWED[...]
[...]OSITION FOR THAT WE ARE SEEKING FOR A TRUSTWORTHY FOREIGN BUSINESS PARTNER WH[...]
[...]S BOI OF MONEY SO THAT HE/SHE MAY INVEST IT FOR US AND KEEP OUR SHARE FOR BANKIN[...]

[...] AND I WILL TAKE 60%, YOU TAKE THE OTHER 40%. NO STRESS ATTACHED, FOR WE HAVE MADE ALL NECESSARY ARRANGEMENT F[...]

[...]ATIC COURIER SERVICE FOR SHIPPING THE MONEY OUT IN ONE LARGE SILVER BOI DECLARING IT AS FAMILY VALUABLES USING DIPLOMATIC IMMUNITY[...]
[...]ETAILS, MY JOB IS TO FIND A GOOD PARTNER THAT WE CAN TRUST TO ASSIST US. CAN I TRUST YOU?

[...]L SIGNIFYING YOUR INTEREST INCLUDING YOUR MOST CONFIDENTIAL TELEPHONE/FAI NUMBERS FOR QUICK COMMUNICATION ALSO YOUR CONTACT DETAILS. THIS BUSINESS IS RISK F[...]
[...]REPLY TO MY PRIVATE MAIL BOI: SGTDELGADOISMAEL@NETSCAPE.NET

Why is Hinduism so confusing ?

Why there are so many gods in Hinduism ?

Why Hindus worship idols ?

Does Hinduism prohibit meat eating ?

What is Hinduism's sacred text ?

What are the marks on the forehead of Hindus ?

Why is Hinduism so complex to understand ?

So could it not be understood by simple minds ?

WHO CAN BECOME A HINDU ?

CAN ONE BE A HINDU ONLY

Hinduism is the religion of one particular land called India, right ?

What is this caste system ?

What is the status of women under Hinduism ?

Who can be a hindu ×

end,
mer
nti-
ing
are
be
rite
tial
her
ore
thin
onal
///
lga.
ndon.net

WORK
Work is my Religion

my Religion

1 Do you get more excited about your work than about family or anything else?

2 Are there times when you can charge through your work and other times when you can't?

3 Do you take work with you to bed? on weekends? on vacation?

4 Is work the activity you like to do best and talk about most?

5 Do you work more than 40 hours a week?

6 Do you turn your hobbies into money-making ventures?

7 Do you take complete responsibility for the outcome of your work efforts?

8 Have your family or friends given up expecting you on time?

9 Do you take on extra work because you are concerned that it won't otherwise get done?

10 Do you underestimate how long a project will take and then rush to complete it?

11 Do you believe that it is okay to work long hours if you love what you are doing?

12 Do you get impatient with people who have other priorities besides work?

13 Are you afraid that if you don't work hard you will lose your job or be a failure?

14 Is the future a constant worry for you even when things are going very well?

15 Do you do things energetically and competitively including play?

16 Do you get irritated when people ask you to stop doing your work in order to do something else?

17 Have your long hours hurt your family or other relationships?

18 Do you think about your work while driving, falling asleep or when others are talking?

19 Do you work or read during meals?

20 Do you believe that more money will solve the other problems in your life?

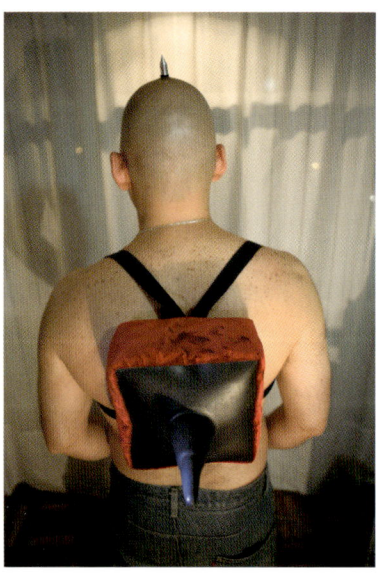

ILLUMINATION

Then, at the age of 35, on the full moon night of May, he s... f what is now known as the Bodhi T... ve by the banks of the river Neranjara... mind in deep but luminous, tranquil... traordinary clarity of such a mind... power generated by states of deep i... his attention to investigate upon the h... universe and life.

...meath the branches
...n a secluded gro-
...d developed his
...tion. Using the ex-
...ts sharp penetrative
...tiffness, he turned
...meanings of mind

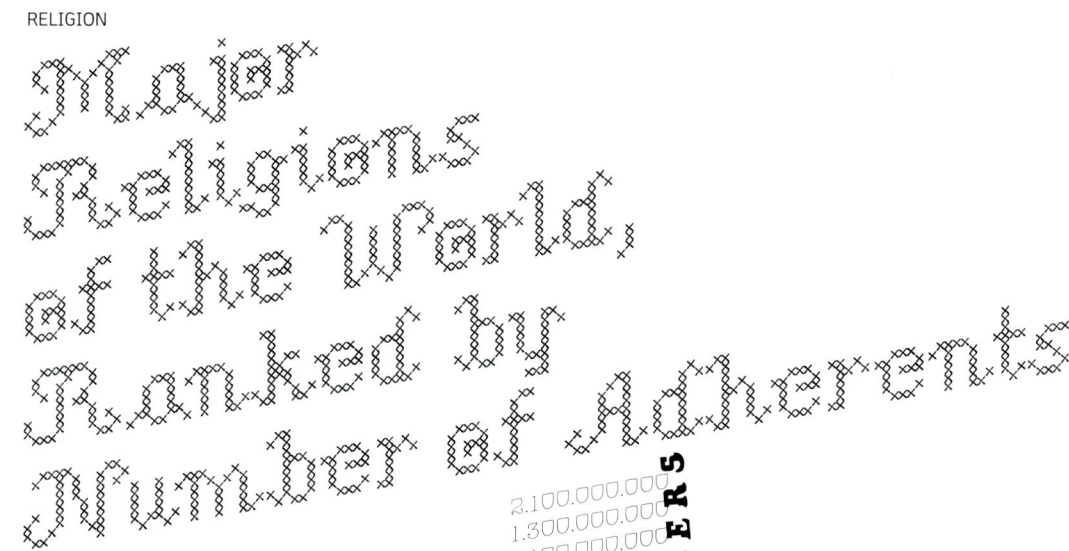

Major Religions of the World, Ranked by Number of Adherents

		NUMBERS NUMBERS	JUST NUMBERS
1	Christianity	2.100.000.000	
2	Islam	1.300.000.000	
3	Secular/Nonreligious/Agnostic/Atheist	1.100.000.000	
4	Hinduism	900.000.000	
5	Chinese traditional religion	394.000.000	
6	Buddhism	376.000.000	
7	primal-indigenous	300.000.000	
8	African Traditional & Diasporic	100.000.000	
9	Sikhism	23.000.000	
10	Juche	19.000.000	
11	Spiritism	15.000.000	
12	Judaism	14.000.000	
13	Baha'i	7.000.000	
14	Jainism	4.200.000	
15	Shinto	4.000.000	
16	Cao Dai	4.000.000	
17	Zoroastrianism	2.600.000	
18	Tenrikyo	2.000.000	
19	Neo-Paganism	1.000.000	
20	Unitarian-Universalism	800.000	
21	Rastafarianism	600.000	
22	Scientology	500.000	

CAPITALISM IS MY RELIGION

THE TEACHING OF THE WORLD RELIGIONS IS DIAMETRICALLY OPPOSED TO THE VALUES OF CAPITALISTIC GLOBALIZATION. THE DEVELOPMENT OF SCIENCE AND TECHNOLOGY CAN IMPROVE HUMAN LIFE, BUT THE CAPITALISTIC VALUES THAT INSPIRE THE SOCIAL RELATIONSHIPS ARE DISASTROUS.

Bonjour .

Avant toute chose, je voudrais m'excuser pour mon intrusion dans votre vie privée.

Je me nomme Mme Marie-laure Anne BILLARD, Cadre au Departement comptabilité et transaction au sein du groupe EcoBank-Côte d'Ivoi

Un compte a été ouvert au sein de notre banque en 1992 et depuis 1994 aucune opération bancaire ne s'est effectuée. Ce compte pr

nos livres, un compte créditeur de 20.8 millions de dollars américains.

Après avoir consulté méticuleusement toutes les archives et les dossiers relatifs à ce compte, je me suis rendu compte que je po ais disposer aisément de

cet argent si je réussissais à le virer sur un compte à l'extérieur du pays.

Le possesseur de ce compte feu Mark Davids, un expatrié,ingénieur en chimie fut directeur de Petrol-Technical Support Services Inc.,il trouva la mort suite à

un accident de la circulation. Personne ne sait à ce jour l'existence de ce compte. Ce compte ne possède aucun autre bénéficiaire aussi bien dans sa famille

que dans son entreprise. Je voudrais transférer l'argent de ce compte sur un compte fiable à l'étranger mais je ne connais personne à l'extérieur.

C'est ainsi que l'idée m'est venue de vous contacter et de vous faire la proposition de virer cette somme sur votre compte banca   rté qui s'offre a vous et

a moi.

Je vous demande de me répondre le plus vite possible pour eventuelle finalisation,tout en sachant compter sur votre dicrétion la plus totale .

cordialement.

Marie-Laure Anne B.

My lord, the bastard died because he got religion!

Don't get me wrong, I'm not suggesting for one second that people don't have the right to believe what they want to believe. They absolutely, positively do. If someone wants to believe that the Moon is made of green cheese, bon appetite. If they want to believe that their God is a tree in the backyard, happy climbing. And if they want to believe that rocks can walk and talk, I couldn't care less. But they're not allowed to pick up that rock and hit me over the head with it simply because I don't share their belief.

This is exactly what Muslims have done, and are doing, with Islam.

When the Twin Towers episode occurred and other Middle-Eastern situations developed, I noticed that my husband grew a beard and started acting very seriously.

When Americans threw rocks at our car for no reason, except that I appeared foreign, he decided that I should go to his small city in the Mideast. It was an industrial city in which I would live with his family while he would stay here to make money.

I grew up in the 70's and felt that there was something very wrong with the spirituality of the West.

I can prove that those who are engaged in terrorism and believe they will go to Paradise having sex with 72 hooris for killing innocent Jews or the Kafir in this world drive their inspiration directly from explicit teachings of Quran. This is what they say too. I can prove the Pakistani soldiers who raped 250.000 Bangali women did exactly what Muhammad did in his wars and told his followers to do in the Quran. I can tell you the brutal and the most heinous practice of stoning as is now practiced in Saudi Arabia and Iran is directly inspired by what the Prophet did and said. I can show you that physical mutilation and cutting the hands of the petty thieves is a teaching of Muhammad while he himself looted all the livelihood of the innocent people killing them and enslaving their wives with absolute immunity.

Now can you tell me what is it that Islam gave you? Have you read the Quran? Have you read the hadith? Do you really know what Muhammad said? You are either a Muslim or a humanist. You cannot have both.

My lord, the bastard died because he got religion!

Do you rea
Muhamm

did the west separate Gov from Church

has globalization become a
religion of money-theism

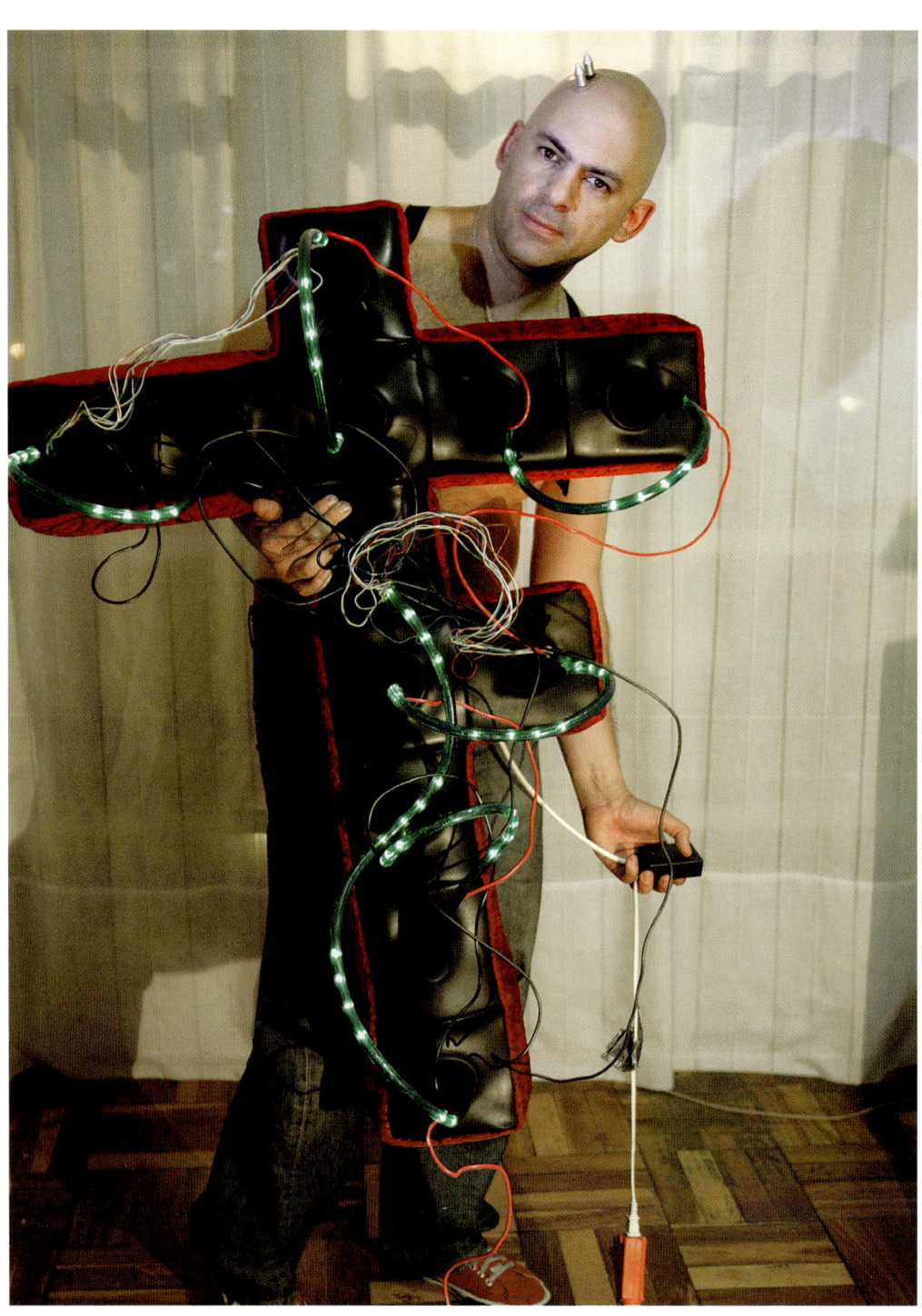

A Perfect Circle
Blind Melon
Jeff Buckley
The Cult
Depeche Mode
Faith No More
Fishbone
The Flaming Lips
Living Colour
Dave Navarro
Nine Inch Nails
Nirvana
Pearl Jam
The Pixies
Primus
Radiohead
The Red Hot Chili Peppers
Henry Rollins
The Smashing Pumpkins
Soundgarden
Spiritualized
Stone Temple Pilots

If you were granted one wish, what would it be?

That all countries would respect the law of animal welfare and rights.

If you were stuck on a Desert Island with one other person (famous or not) whom would you choose?

My dad, cause he's a real survivor with a lot of experience in life.

What is your message to all the other Miss World contestants?

Be proud of who you are because you all mean something to someone, and take nothing for granted.

You're judging the final five contestants, which question would you ask the finalists?

IS BEAUTY IMPORTANT IN LIFE?

THE LOVE
OF SLOWNESS

DIE LIEBE
ZUR LANGSAMKEIT

RADEK KNAPP

1. An era continues to search to be defined

Ten years ago I met a woman, and we ended up becoming pen pals, but eventually, over time, our friendship ebbed away. Just recently, I ran into her on the street, and as I was giving her my e-mail address and she was giving me hers, it struck us that we had reunited in a new era. We went to a café to talk this over, but the more we brooded, the clearer it became that our era could not be reduced to any single common denominator. The only thing we could agree on was that our new era was the fastest paced in the history of humankind. At the same time, we could not deny it a certain sense of humor. Our era has, after all, given us a sheep named Dolly, and made the wealthiest man in the world out of a computer programmer.

To our extreme chagrin, however, we also realized that we thirty-somethings had within an extremely short period of time been degraded to contemporary witnesses, requiring us to explain things to today's teenagers in a grandfatherly fashion about the way things were "back then." Back when we were young, for instance, there were these cameras, which you had to insert a roll of film into, and then you had to take this roll of film to a special shop in order to get it developed. There were also these things called home telephones. You couldn't take them with you, or even put them in your pocket. They were fixed to one spot and certain models even had a dial where you had to insert your finger and turn it as far as it would go. Incidentally, rotary dialing could get quite painful, and you could never be entirely certain that you weren't in fact ringing up the wrong person. But, then again, at the time, you could find a contraption called a telephone booth on nearly every street corner, and enclosed in these small creations you could make your necessary phone calls. Incidentally, it was one of these booths that saved a character's life in a thriller by Alfred Hitchcock (a motion-picture director of old).

Ten years ago, at parties, we listened to smash hits by artist Methuselahs with names like Madonna, George Michael and Prince. These rock stars, by the way, used real instruments on stage, such as guitars, and never used chain saws like some of their successors today. Music was recorded on LPs, which, today, are generally referred to as "vinyl". Today, these are kept right next to all the other primitive precursors to the CD format, most likely so that teenagers will have an easier time finding them at the museum.

After we had finished talking about our "back thens", my friend made an interesting discovery. Today, even how we define the word "fortune" has changed. Recently, someone had asked for her cell phone number, and she had been forced to admit that she didn't have one. This reaped an envious look from her interlocutor, who quickly replied: "You are so fortunate!" That's when we both let out a sigh of relief: the new era did have a common denominator after all. It has never been easier to feel fortunate. Or, maybe, it would be more accurate to say: it has never been easier to feel fortunate so quickly.

2. How Jeff thought he was a character in a video game

In physics, velocity is measured as the time rate a body needs to get from A to B. If this "body" happens to be a creature in possession of consciousness, such as a human being, velocity gains a psychological dimension. A creature not only physically moves within a given space, but simultaneously is in the firm belief of being "moved" emotionally by the change of position. You can already see this happening in ten-year-olds busy playing with their Playstations, and the phenomenon can end with the motorcyclist, who insists on continuing to accelerate although the bike is already going 260 km/h.

Certainly, fast processes in today's society are useful and shouldn't be discarded as unnecessary. The quickness with which news can be transmitted has been known to save lives and hinder catastrophes. Speed's benevolence can be seen in the rate at which special medicines affect our bodies, and surgical operations are able to be carried out. All of us have probably experienced this first hand in some way.

Due to the modernization of our factories, the working hours of the average citizen in the Western world has been reduced by half. Our society would most likely appear to someone from the Middle Ages as a sort of garden of paradise. The highly deceitful nature of this idea, however, can be discovered very quickly just by opening a newspaper.

How, for instance, can it be possible that modern laboratories of the 21st century can not only produce a range of lifesaving medicines, but also gives us the means to practice euthanasia, which has become legal in the democratic and modern country of the Netherlands? Why do 25% of all Americans and Europeans, who have more free time in this era than ever before, suffer from chronic stress syndrome? In Japan, a social stratum of workaholics has been growing steadily for years. The careers of these people often end suddenly in "karoshi", a phenomenon which literally translates as "death from overwork".

Is it possible that the very speed that we rely on to cope with the everyday isn't merely a "side effect" produced by our modern society, but, in fact, much much more? Is it possible that speed itself has become a drug? A drug made all the more treacherous because it isn't defined as one? Researchers have actually found that the impact it has on the brain's reward system, which has definitely been linked to "the need for speed", is equal to that which follows heroin use. And all you have to do is observe some teenager frantically trying to retrieve a jingling cell phone from a pant pocket to distinctly recall the concept of the conditioned reflex as demonstrated by Pavlov and his dog. According to statistics, a child in the West spends an average of 6 hours in front of his or her Playstation or the television set each day. The fact that this results in physical, as well as psychological disorders is an obvious notion. Childhood, once considered a safe and harmonious haven for our youth, has turned into a training camp, where the children have to be very strong in order to come through the phase reasonably unharmed. Children's diseases, things like the measles and scarlet fever have been replaced by more puzzling phenomenons such as convulsive epileptic seizures and ADHD (attention-deficit/hyperactivity disorder). The unfortunate child affected by this syndrome is restless and unable to sit still. A few years ago, the story of a five-year-old New York boy named Jeff splashed onto papers across the globe. Some considered his fate a tragedy resulting from a series of unfortunate events, while others felt it had all been a lamentable accident. When Jeff came home from kindergarten on this ominous afternoon, he did what he always did. He took out a package of frozen french fries, heated them in the microwave, and sat down to play his favorite video game. After an hour or so, he was seized suddenly by the urge to imitate his favorite character, and so he opened the window of his room, which was on the 20th floor of his apartment building. Expecting to land safely on the street below to then catapult himself up onto the building across the way, like his favorite video game character, Jeff jumped right out of the window without sensing the slightest fear. He died on impact. We can only guess what Jeff's childhood might have been like fifty years ago, but having grown up in that era, he would likely still be alive today. And he would also probably have taught his children what our era has simply failed to get through to us all: the faster we pursue paradise, the faster it moves away.

3. How to make gold out of shit

In the 1980s, the author Sten Nadolny completed a novel called *The Discovery of Slowness*. The title says it all. After reading this book, it suddenly became clear to many people that slowness isn't a handicap, but a state in which reality can be experienced to the fullest. It was no accident that a writer, of all people, was needed to bring this notion back into the consciousness of the population. Artists (and I'm not referring to actors or pop stars whose careers have an expiration date comparable to that of banana yogurt) know out of their own experience, that speed is fluid and can stimulate performance. "Good things take time", as the saying goes. René Magritte once said it much better. Responding to a question on how long he needed in order to complete a painting, he replied: "The painting itself takes me a few weeks, but the idea behind it takes years." Even in the automobile manufacturing industry, where speed is key, experts are aware that an automobile assembled in record-time will have more errors than one assembled during the proven time needed. Renowned scientists, who draw on the same kind of intuition as artists do, also know that slowness is the fastest route to success. There was no better place for Albert Einstein to sit and brood on the speed of light than in a sleepy Swiss patent office. And Niels Bohr is said to have dreamt up the theory of the atom while taking a little nap one peaceful afternoon.

In order to demonstrate what happens when velocity is given free reign, the Italian artist Piero Manzoni in the 1960s produced and tinned ninety cans of shit. He then signed the labels of the cans and drew everyone's attention to the large lettering explaining what was inside. The revolutionary inscription read: "Artist's Shit". Today, only a few cans are still intact, because many art buyers, who, back then, paid around $500 for one, simply couldn't resist taking a look inside. The average price of a "Manzoni can" has, in the meantime, rocketed to $50,000. If you're fortunate, it is still possible to acquire one at auction at Sotheby's. It is very well feasible that they will one day reach the price of a Renoir. Will it make us millionaires? Probably not. But how was this speedy increase in worth possible? Initially, Manzoni's cans were the laughing stock of the art world, and yet their value steadily went up. Though everyone knew what was inside, an entire armada of managers, critics and art agents, in the wink of an eye, managed to turn the "Manzoni can" into a work of art.

A hundred years ago, a "Manzoni can" would have merely become a footnote in the history of art made by an eccentric artist. Today, it has cult value. And deservedly so. Because, ultimately, Manzoni was able to triumph over his very own art agents. His cans are proof that in our era something very unique is possible, something which the Middle Ages unsuccessfully tried to create: the sorcerer's stone – the art of turning nothing into gold. Well, in this case, maybe not exactly nothing.

4. Protect the human brain

One-hundred years ago, every human being could rest assured that when they departed from this world, it would be from the same one they had arrived to. Forty years ago, this assurance became history. It was then that human beings began, bit by bit, to cross certain borders without even realizing it. One of the most ominous of these "border crossings" was entering into the world of consumerism. This transition not only came to pass in a totally painless fashion, but the road up ahead was to be paved with even more pleasant things, which, for the most part, would be nearly impossible to pass up. The problem is that today's consumer is in the possession of a brain that looks and functions not much differently from the one of 100,000 years ago. And this ancient brain may have discovered the microchip and the semiconductor, but it is unable to consume the fruits its labors without, in the long run, doing at least some harm to itself.

One of the most fundamental physiological characteristics of the human organ of thought is the inability to process an excess number of stimuli. There is a natural built-in blocking effect which serves to protect our minds; it is meant to keep the brain from suffering a nervous breakdown. Nevertheless, this border is crossed shamelessly. Especially by advertisers. A creative director working for a big advertising agency recently made the proud announcement that his company was consciously working on finding a way to allow for quicker infiltration of the brain, so as to increase the number of stimuli it can uptake, thereby serving the customer better. This man should be thrown in jail, but instead he earns a fortune.

A further border of the brain which human beings have crossed much too quickly is in relation to the loss of territory. The English anthropologist Desmond Morris calculated that during the last 2 million years around 100 people lived in a space roughly the size of New York. Today 7 million people must manage in that same space. In the animal kingdom, this kind of population surplus results in mass suicide (observed in lemmings), for instance, or finds regulation in periodic outbreaks of epidemics. Despite numerous theories maintaining that the epidemics of the 20th century are increased armed warfare and AIDS, this does not change the fact that human beings have lost their original territory forever.

Despite a sense of pessimism, it would be premature to paint a picture of doom and give up on our era. It has, after all, produced quite a fine collection of optimists. Hoimar von Ditfurth's terse reply to the question of what he would do if he knew that the world would end tomorrow was: "I'd go outside today and plant a little apple tree." The Polish film director Roman Polanski even suggested that on doomsday he would set out and try to find the best place to put his camera.

Besides, complaining about the era in which one lives is almost considered good taste. Seneca remarked in AD 50 that he lived in a "greedy and chaotic time period, where people only thought of money". At the end of the Renaissance period, Giordano Bruno, whose theories today would only have reaped fame and glory, was punished by his contemporaries and suffered death at the stake.

It is fairly improbable that fellow-creatures today will suddenly get the urge to renounce their "need for speed" and usher in a new era — an era of slowness. But much could be gained by listening to the warnings that can be heard around the globe: "Save the ozone layer". and "Stop pollution". One further warning might be in order: "Protect the human brain." Especially from itself.

1. Eine Epoche sucht nach einem Namen

Vor zehn Jahren traf ich eine Frau, mit der ich anschließend viele Briefe tauschte. Die Freundschaft verebbte und ich traf sie wieder kürzlich auf der Straße. Sie gab mir ihre Mailadresse und ich ihr meine. Uns wurde klar, daß wir uns in einer neuen Epoche wiederfanden. Wir gingen in ein Kaffeehaus und unterhielten uns darüber. Je mehr wir nachgrübelten, desto klarer wurde uns, daß unsere Epoche keinen gemeinsamen Nenner hatte. Sicher war nur, daß sie die schnellebigste in der Geschichte der Menschheit war, wobei man ihr einen gewissen Sinn für Humor nicht absprechen konnte. Schließlich hat sie der Welt ein Schaf namens Dolly geschenkt und einen Programmierer zum reichsten Mann der Welt gemacht.

Persönlich entrüstete uns aber am meisten, daß sie uns Mitdreißigjährige in kürzester Zeit zu Zeitzeugen degradiert hatte, die inzwischen in großväterlicher Manier den Teenagern von „früher" berichten könnten. Da gab es „früher" zum Beispiel Photoapparate, in die man die Filme einlegen und dann in einen speziellen Laden zur „Entwicklung" bringen mußte. Es gab Telefone, die man nicht mitnehmen oder in die Tasche stecken konnte. Sie standen fest an einem Platz und einige Modelle hatten sogar eine Wählscheibe, in die man den Finger hineinsteckte und bis zum Anschlag drehte. Es war gelegentlich richtig schmerzvoll und man war sich nie sicher, ob man die richtige Nummer gewählt hatte, aber dafür gab es an jeder Straßenecke kleine Kabinen, von wo man anrufen konnte. Man nannte sie Telefonzellen. Eines dieser Dinger rettete übrigens mal einer Figur im Horrorfilm von Alfred Hitchcock (ein altertümlicher Filmemacher) sogar das Leben. Wenn wir vor zehn Jahren auf eine Party gingen, machten gerade die Songs von solchen Methusalems wie Madonna, George Michael oder Prince Furore. Diese Rockstars trugen übrigens damals auf der Bühne Gitarren und andere Instrumente und nicht wie ihre heutigen Nachfolger Kettensägen. Die Musik kam aus einer LP, die man heute als „Vinylplatte" bezeichnet. Wahrscheinlich damit die Teenager sie leichter im Museum finden, wo sie neben den vielen anderen primitiven Vorläufern der CD ausgestellt werden.

Und als wir unser „Früher" durch hatten, machte meine Bekannte eine interessante Entdeckung. Heute wird sogar bereits der Begriff des Glücks anders definiert. Als sie neulich jemand nach ihrer Handynummer fragte, mußte sie zugeben, daß sie kein Handy besitze. Sie erntete einen neidischen Blick und dann folgte die Antwort: „Du bist ein richtiger Glückspilz." Und da atmeten wir endlich auf: Die neue Epoche hatte doch einen gemeinsamen Nenner. Es war noch nie so leicht glücklich zu werden wie heute. Oder besser gesagt: so schnell.

2. Wie Jeff eine Comicfigur nachahmte

In der Physik bezeichnet man die Geschwindigkeit als jenes Tempo, welches ein fester Körper braucht um von A nach B zu gelangen. Ist dieser „feste Körper" ein Wesen mit Bewußtsein, wie der Mensch, bekommt die Geschwindigkeit auch eine psychologische Dimension. Das Wesen wird nicht nur durch den Raum bewegt, sondern glaubt gleichzeitig von der Bewegung „ergriffen" worden zu sein. Das beginnt bei einem Zehnjährigen, der Playstation spielt, und endet bei einem Motorradfahrer, der bei 260 Kilometer pro Stunde das Gaspedal noch weiter drückt.

Gewiß, der Nutzen von schnellen Prozessen in der heutigen Gesellschaft ist nicht von der Hand zu weisen. Die rasche Übermittlung von Nachrichten hat schon so manches Leben gerettet oder eine Katastrophe verhindert. Die wohltuende Schnelligkeit, mit der bestimmte Medikamente auf unseren Körper wirken oder Eingriffe durchgeführt werden, hat jeder von uns schon mal an sich selbst ausprobieren können. Und die Modernisierung unserer Fabriken hat die Arbeitszeit eines Durchschnittsbürgers in der westlichen Welt halbiert. Unsere Gesellschaft müßte auf einen Besucher aus dem Mittelalter wie ein paradiesischer Garten wirken. Aber, daß es ein falsches Paradies ist, wird spätestens klar, wenn man die Zeitung aufschlägt:

Wie ist es zum Beispiel möglich, daß die modernen Labors des einundzwanzigsten Jahrhunderts nicht nur lebensrettende Medikamente produzieren, sondern auch Euthanasiemittel, die inzwischen in einem demokratischen und modernen Staat wie Holland ganz offiziell angewendet werden? Warum leidet bereits ein Viertel der Amerikaner und Europäer, die über so viel Freizeit wie noch nie verfügen, am chronischen Streßsyndrom? In Japan wächst seit mehreren Jahren kontinuierlich eine Schicht von workaholics heran, deren Laufbahn mit „karoshi" – dem Tod am Arbeitsplatz endet.

Kann es sein, daß die Geschwindigkeit, mit der wir unseren Alltag bewältigen, nicht nur ein „Nebenprodukt" unserer Gesellschaft ist, sondern doch mehr? Ist sie womöglich eine Droge, deren heimtückische Eigenschaft darin besteht, nicht als solche erkannt werden zu können? Die Wissenschaftler haben tatsächlich herausgefunden, daß der Geschwindigkeitsrausch genauso wie Heroin im menschlichen Gehirn das „Belohnungszentrum" stimuliert. Man braucht nur einem Teeanger zuzusehen, wie er verzweifelt nach einem klingelnden Handy in seiner Hosentasche wühlt, um sich an den bedingten Reflex des Pawlowschen Hundes zu erinnern. Laut Statistik verbringt heute ein westliches Kind im Schnitt sechs Stunden vor der Playstation oder dem Fernseher. Daß es davon physische und psychische Störungen davonträgt ist geradezu logisch. Die Kindheit, einst der Hort der Harmonie, ist zu einem Trainingscamp geworden, das nur die Stärksten halbwegs unbeschadet überstehen. Kinderkrankheiten wie Masern oder Scharlach wurden von unerklärlichen Epilepsieanfällen oder dem ADHD (Attention Deficit Hyperactivity Disorder) Syndrom abgelöst. Der Unglücksrabe, der von letzterem befallen wird, kann weder sitzen noch stehen, er muß dauernd in Bewegung bleiben. Vor einigen Jahren machte weltweit der Fall des fünfjährigen Jeff aus New York Schlagzeilen. Für die einen war die Tragödie auf eine Verkettung von unglücklichen Umständen zurückzuführen, für andere war es nur ein bedauerlicher Unfall. Als Jeff an jenem verhängnisvollen Nachmittag vom Kindergarten nach Hause kam, tat er das, was er schon auswendig beherrschte. Er holte sich eine Packung Pommes Frites, die er sich selbst in der Mikrowelle aufwärmte und setzte sich vor sein Videospiel. Nach einer Stunde überkam ihn die Lust, seine Lieblingscomicfigur aus dem Video nachzuahmen. Zu diesem Zweck öffnete Jeff das Fenster seines Kinderzimmers, welches sich im zwanzigsten Stock eines Hochhauses befand. In der sicheren Erwartung, unten auf der Straße anzukommen, um sich anschließend genauso wie seine Lieblingscomicfigur auf das gegenüberliegende Gebäude zu katapultieren, sprang Jeff ohne jegliche Anwandlung von Angst herunter. Er war auf der Stelle tot. Man kann nur mutmaßen, wie Jeffs Kindheit vor fünfzig Jahren ausgesehen hätte. Aber er wäre mit großer Wahrscheinlichkeit heute noch am Leben. Dann hätte er seinen Kindern bestimmt das beigebracht, was ihm unsere Epoche unmöglich beibringen konnte: Je schneller man einem Paradies hinterher jagt, desto schneller entfernt es sich von einem.

3. Wie man aus Kacke Gold macht

In den achtziger Jahren des zwanzigsten Jahrhunderts schrieb Sten Nadolny den Roman „ Die Entdeckung der Langsamkeit". Der Titel hatte es in sich. Auf einmal wurde vielen Menschen klar, daß Langsamkeit kein Handikap ist, sondern ein Zustand, in dem sich die Wirklichkeit intensiver und bewußter erleben läßt. Es war kein Zufall, daß ausgerechnet ein Schriftsteller an diese Selbstverständlichkeit wieder erinnern mußte. Künstler (dabei ist nicht die Rede von etwaigen Schauspielern oder Popstars, deren Karrieren das Verfallsdatum eines Bananenjoghurts haben) wissen aus eigener Erfahrung, daß Geschwindigkeit kein Fluidum ist, welches große Leistungen fördert. „Gut Ding Weile braucht" heißt es im Volksmund. René Magritte brachte es etwas eleganter auf den Punkt. Er antwortete auf die Frage, wie lange er für ein Bild brauche: „Für die Ausführung ein paar Wochen, aber für die Idee Jahre." Sogar die Autoindustrie, der es nicht schnell genug gehen kann, weiß, daß ein Wagen, der unter einem bestimmten Zeitlimit zusammengebaut wird, mehr Fehler aufweist als jener, der sich an das Limit hielt. Auch unter großen Wissenschaftlern, die auf der gleichen intuitiven Basis wie Künstler arbeiten, ist die Langsamkeit sogar häufig der schnellste Weg zum Erfolg. Nirgendwo anders konnte Albert Einstein so gut über die Lichtgeschwindigkeit nachgrübeln, wie in den verschlafenen Räumlichkeiten des Schweizer Patentamtes. Und Niels Bohr erträumte gar das Atommodell bei einem ruhigen Nachmittagsnickerchen.

Um zu zeigen was passiert, wenn man der Geschwindigkeit freien Lauf läßt, setzte der italienische Künstler Piero Manzoni in den sechziger Jahren folgende Idee in die Tat um. Er füllte neunzig Dosen mit seinen eigenen Exkrementen. Dann verschloß er sie hermetisch, signierte sie und verwies mit der großen Aufschrift auf den Inhalt: „Artists Shit" lautete die revolutionäre Aufschrift. Heute sind nur noch wenige intakte Dosen vorhanden. Viele Käufer, die damals das Kunstwerk um etwa 500 Dollar erstanden haben, konnten einfach nicht widerstehen hineinzuschauen. Inzwischen liegt der Preis einer Manzoni-Dose bei 50 Tausend Dollar. Man kann sie noch mit viel Glück bei Sotheby's ersteigern. Es ist nicht auszuschließen, daß sie irgendwann mal den Preis eines Renoirs erreicht. Können wir auch Millionäre werden? Eher kaum. Warum war es also doch möglich? Am Anfang wurden die Dosen von Manzoni als eine Lachnummer abgestempelt und doch begann sehr schnell ihr Wert zu steigen. Obwohl jeder wußte, was darinnen war, schritt eine Armee aus Agenten, Kritikern und Impressarios zur Tat und machte aus der Manzoni-Dose im Handumdrehen ein Kunstwerk.

Vor hundert Jahren wäre die Manzoni-Dose nur eine skurrile Fußnote in der Geschichte der Kunst. Heute ist sie Kult. Und durchaus verdient. Denn am Ende hat Manzoni seine Impressarios selbst überlistet. Seine Dose zeigt, daß in unserer Epoche etwas möglich ist, wonach man schon seit dem Mittelalter vergeblich gesucht hat: Der Stein der Weisen, oder die Kunst, aus nichts Gold zu machen. Nun, vielleicht nicht ganz aus nichts.

4. Schützt das menschliche Gehirn

Noch vor hundert Jahren konnte so gut wie jeder Mensch davon ausgehen, daß er dieselbe Welt verlassen wird, die er angetroffen hat. Vor etwa vierzig Jahren war damit endgültig Schluss. Von da an begann in kurzen Abständen der Mensch eine Grenze nach der anderen zu überschreiten, ohne sich dessen überhaupt bewußt zu werden. Eine der verhängnisvollsten dieser „Grenzüberschreitungen" war der Eintritt in die Welt des Konsumenten. Dieser Übergang ging nicht nur schmerzlos vor sich, er war auch mit so vielen angenehmen Begleiterscheinungen gepflastert, daß es kaum jemanden gab, der sich ihm entziehen konnte. Das Problem liegt darin, daß der Konsument von heute im Kopf ein Gehirn trägt, das biologisch gesehen identisch ist mit dem von vor hunderttausend Jahren. Dieses hunderttausend Jahre alte Gehirn mag zwar einen Mikrochip und den Halbleiter erfunden haben, kann aber die Früchte seiner Arbeit niemals konsumieren können, ohne dabei auf Dauer Schaden zu erleiden. Eine der fundamentalen, physiologischen Eigenschaften des menschlichen Denkorgans ist die Fähigkeit nur eine begrenzte Anzahl von Reizen aufzunehmen. Diese natürliche Aufnahmegrenze, die als Schutzmaßnahme gedacht ist, soll verhindern, daß das menschliche Gehirn seinen Dienst versagt. Dennoch wird diese Grenze notorisch überschritten. Vor allem von Werbeprofis. Kürzlich verkündete ein „Creative Director" einer großen Reklameagentur stolz, daß seine Firma daran arbeite bewußt diese Schwelle im Hirn noch schneller zu unterwandern, um den Konsumenten besser zu erreichen. Dieser Mann müßte eigentlich ins Gefängnis gesteckt werden, statt dessen verdient er ein Vermögen.

Eine weitere Grenze, die der Mensch viel zu schnell überschritt, hat mit dem Verlust des Territoriums zu tun. Der englische Anthropologe Desmond Morris rechnete aus, daß in den letzten zwei Millionen Jahren auf einer Fläche von New York an die hundert Menschen lebten. Jetzt sind es sieben Millionen, die nebeneinander auskommen müssen. Im Tierreich wird ein Populationsüberschuß zum Beispiel durch Massenselbstmord (wie bei Lemmingen) oder periodisch auftretende Seuchen reguliert. Auch wenn Theorien auftauchen, daß·die vermehrten Waffenkonflikte des zwanzigsten Jahrhunderts sowie die neuen Epidemien wie Aids dasselbe Regulationsprinzip aufweisen, ändert es nichts daran, daß der Mensch ein für alle Mal sein ursprüngliches Territorium verloren hat.

Doch bei allem Pessimismus wäre es zu früh, ein apokalyptisches Szenario zu entwerfen und unsere Epoche zu begraben. Sie hat viel Gutes hervorgebracht, wie zum Beispiel eine große Anzahl an Optimisten. Hoimar von Ditfurth antwortete auf die Frage, was er täte, wenn er erfahren würde, daß morgen die Welt untergeht mit einem knappen: „Ich würde noch heute ein Apfelbäumchen pflanzen." Der polnische Filmemacher Roman Polanski meinte sogar, daß er am Tag des jüngsten Gerichts nach dem Platz suchen würde, wo er die Kamera am besten hinstellt. Darüber hinaus gehörte es immer schon zum guten Ton, über die eigene Epoche zu meckern. Seneca bezeichnete 50 nach Christi seine Zeit auch als eine „habgierige und chaotische Zeitperiode, wo Menschen nur ans Geld denken". Giordano Bruno wurde sogar am Ende der Renaissance von seinen Zeitgenossen für Behauptungen, die ihm heute Ruhm und Ansehen gebracht hätten, mit dem Scheiterhaufen bestraft.

Es ist zwar unwahrscheinlich, daß unsere Mitmenschen auf einmal den Wunsch verspüren, dem Geschwindigkeitsrausch zu entsagen und eine Epoche der Langsamkeit einzuleiten. Aber es wäre schon viel gewonnen, wenn zu Warnrufen, die heute die Runde um den Erdball machen wie zum Beispiel „Rettet die Ozonschicht", oder „Reduziert die Umweltverschmutzung" man einen weiteren dazustellen würde: „Schützt das menschliche Gehirn." In erster Linie vor sich selbst.

WE HAVE THE POSSIBILITY TO DO IT YOU CAN COP IT

IF YOU LIKE DESIGN YOU CAN DO IT!!

I BELIEVE IN MY WORK

MY TIME.

50% MONEY WORK
50% MY OWN STUFF

MY MOTHER LIKES IT!
YOU THINK IT IS PORN? MY MOTHER?

WE ARE ADULTS WE ARE ADULTS
WE ARE ADULTS WE ARE ADULTS
WE ARE ADULTS WE ARE ADULTS
WE ARE ADULTS

IT IS FUNNY
IT IS FUNNY
IT IS FUNNY
IT IS FUNNY

LATEX

LATEX

LATEX

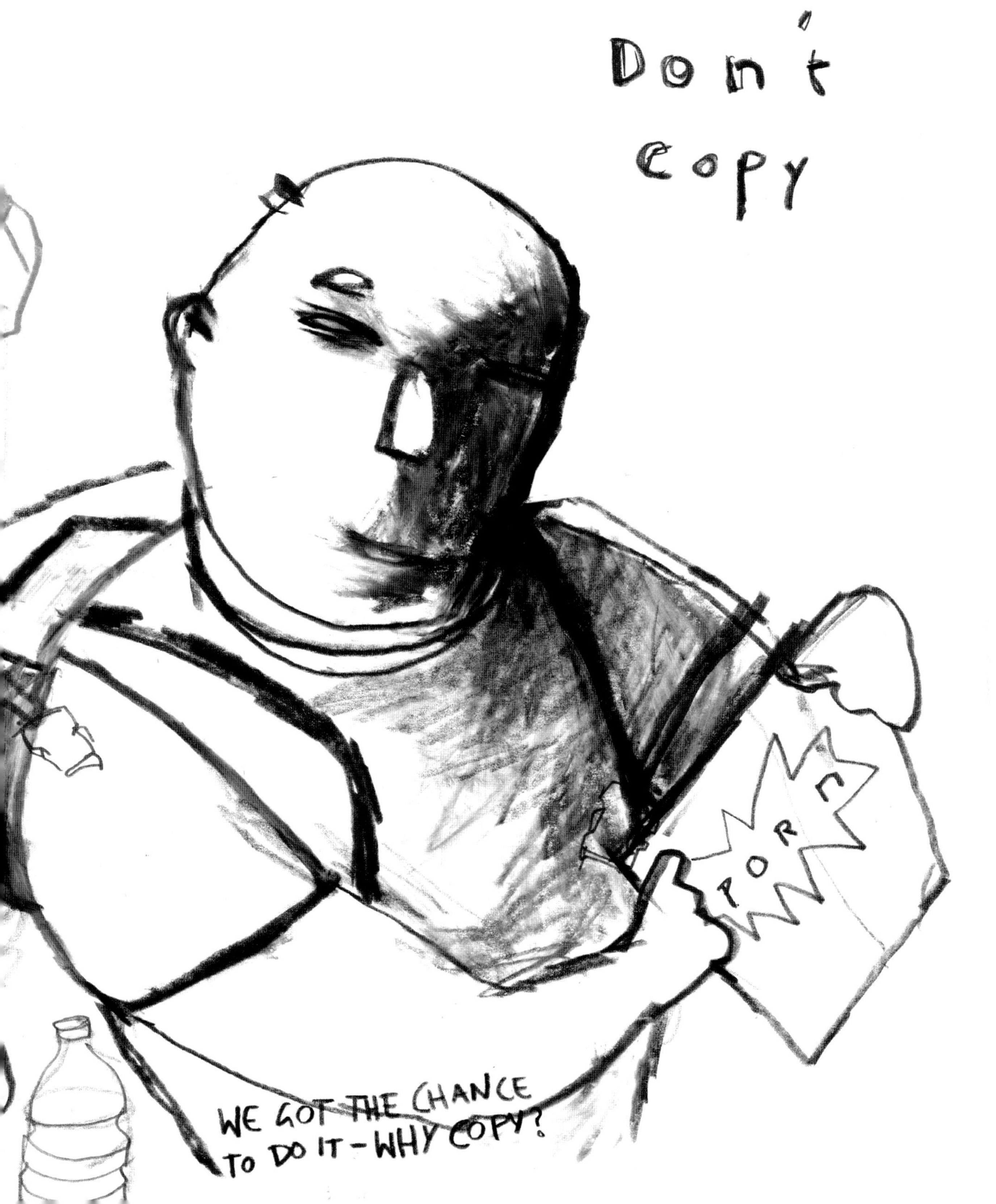
Don't copy
WE GOT THE CHANCE TO DO IT - WHY COPY?

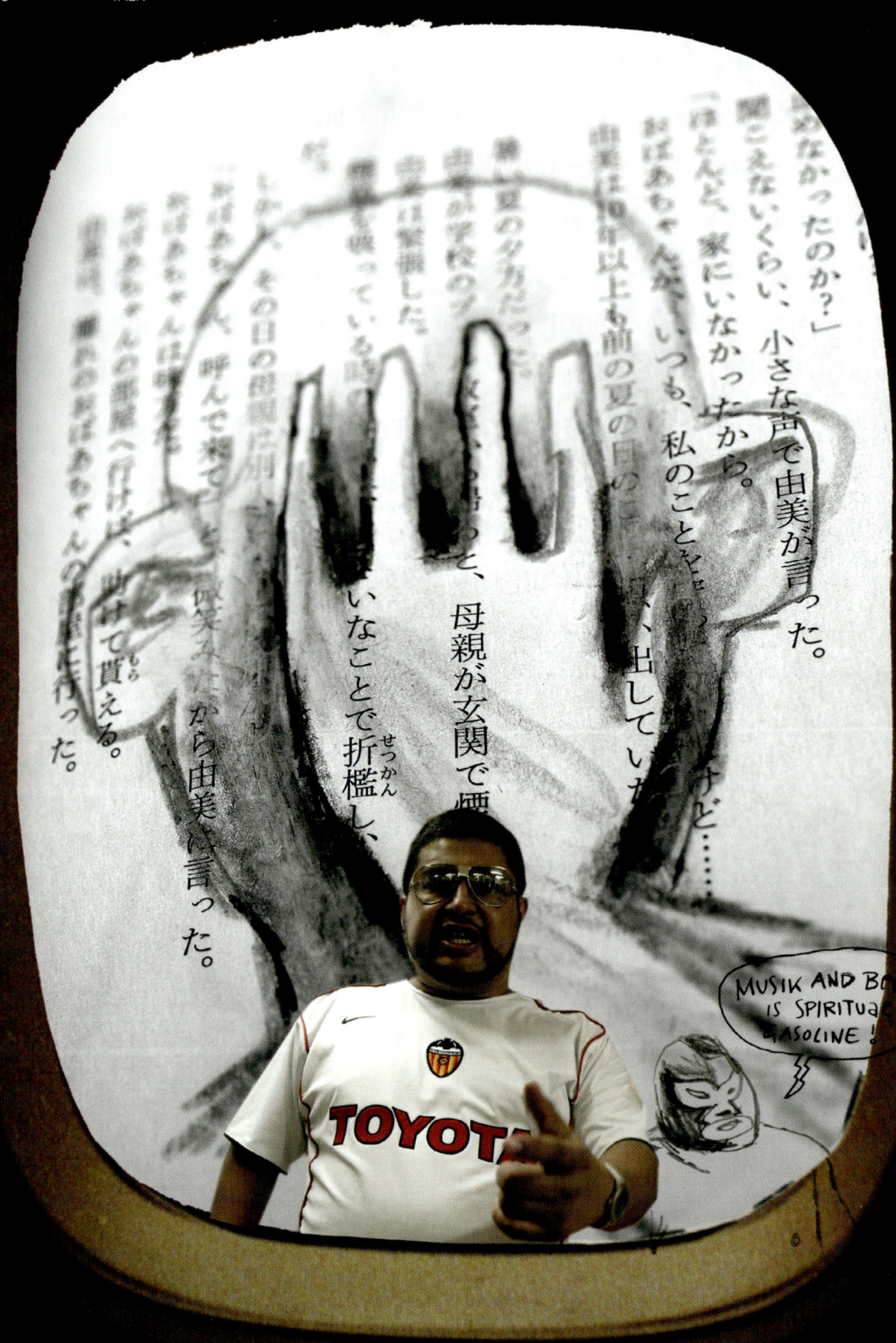

FAKIR

DR. LATEX   ESCOBAR   RAPHAKIR   1000 CHANGOS   JAVO

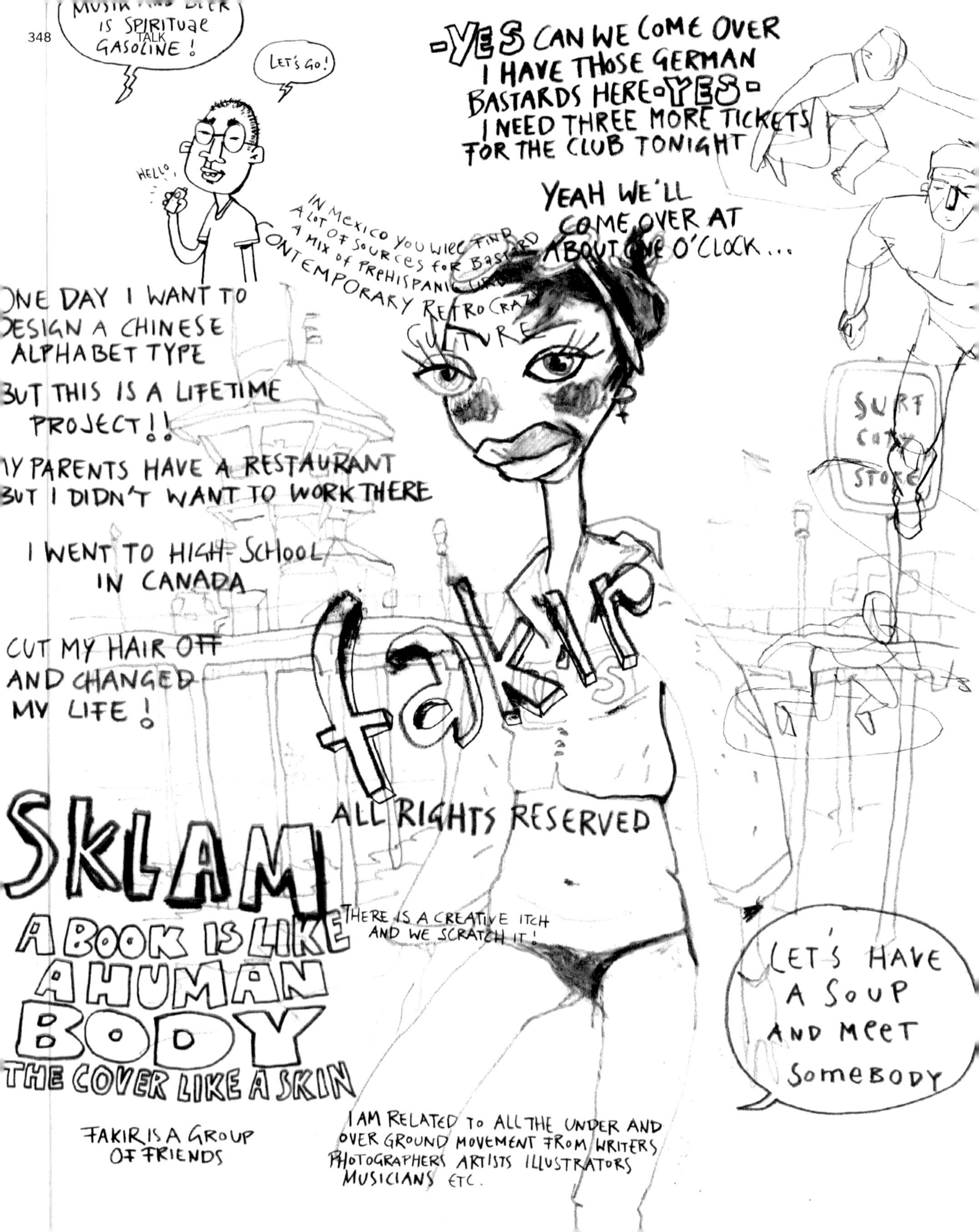

MUSIK AND BEER IS SPIRITUAL TALK GASOLINE!

LET'S GO!

HELLO.

-YES CAN WE COME OVER I HAVE THOSE GERMAN BASTARDS HERE -YES- I NEED THREE MORE TICKETS FOR THE CLUB TONIGHT

IN MEXICO YOU WILL FIND A LOT OF SOURCES FOR BASTARD A MIX OF PREHISPANIC AND CONTEMPORARY RETRO CRAZY CULTURE

YEAH WE'LL COME OVER AT ABOUT ONE O'CLOCK...

ONE DAY I WANT TO DESIGN A CHINESE ALPHABET TYPE

BUT THIS IS A LIFETIME PROJECT!!

MY PARENTS HAVE A RESTAURANT BUT I DIDN'T WANT TO WORK THERE

I WENT TO HIGH SCHOOL IN CANADA

CUT MY HAIR OFF AND CHANGED MY LIFE!

SURF CITY STORE

fakir

SKLAM
A BOOK IS LIKE A HUMAN BODY THE COVER LIKE A SKIN

THERE IS A CREATIVE ITCH AND WE SCRATCH IT!

LET'S HAVE A SOUP AND MEET SOMEBODY

FAKIR IS A GROUP OF FRIENDS

I AM RELATED TO ALL THE UNDER AND OVER GROUND MOVEMENT FROM WRITERS PHOTOGRAPHERS ARTISTS ILLUSTRATORS MUSICIANS ETC.

I STUDY AT THE LI PO CHUN UNITED WORLD COLLEGE OF HONG KONG

I SHARE MY ROOM WITH THREE OTHER GIRLS EACH FROM A DIFFERENT CONTINENT

SUFFERG

AFTER NINE MONTHS OF EMPLOYMENT I OPENED MY OWN OFFICE WHEN I AM 40 I'LL GO TO EUROPE RETIRE FROM WORK STUDY DESIGN AND DRIVE A BMW

EINES TAGES GEHE ICH NACH COSTA RICA...

ICH BIN GEGANGEN UM ALLEINE ZU SEIN ICH HABE SCHNELL GLEICHGESINNTE GETROFFEN!

WE ARE ALL IN ALL OVER 80 DIFFEREN NATIONALITIES IT IS AN INTERNATIONAL MULTICULTURAL PROJECT

I BIN US REUTLINGÄ WIE GEHTS SO IN DEUTSCHLAND? MEIN RICHTER WAR IN ORNUNG ER HAT GESAGT ICH SOLL T MEINER FRAU BESSER EINEN LANGEN HERLAUB MACHEN IR SIND NICHT WIEDER GEKOMMEN!

ES IST SPANNEND ZU SEHEN WIE EIN JUNGER NIGERIANER ZUM ERSTEN MAL IN SEINEM LEBEN MC DONALDS BETRITT UND SEIN AFGHANISCHER FREUND DIE BEATLES ALS NEUE BAND ENTDECKT!!

DAS IST EIN KOMISCHES LAND HIER ALLES IST BIG GELD IST DAS ABSOLUT EINZIGE WAS ZÄHLT

TINKA

WHY SHOULD I HAVE A SMALL TV I WANT A BIG ONE!!!! oooo

MEINE ENGSTEN FREUNDE HIER KOMMEN AUS JAPAN VENEZUELA BRASILIEN NORWEGEN RUSSLAND PAKISTAN ISRAEL PALESTINA DEM NIGER SÜDAFRIKA TSCHECHIEN DEN FIDJI- INSELN UND KANADA?

NACH DEUTSCHLAND ZURÜCK WILL ICH NICHT. WAS SOLL ICH DA?

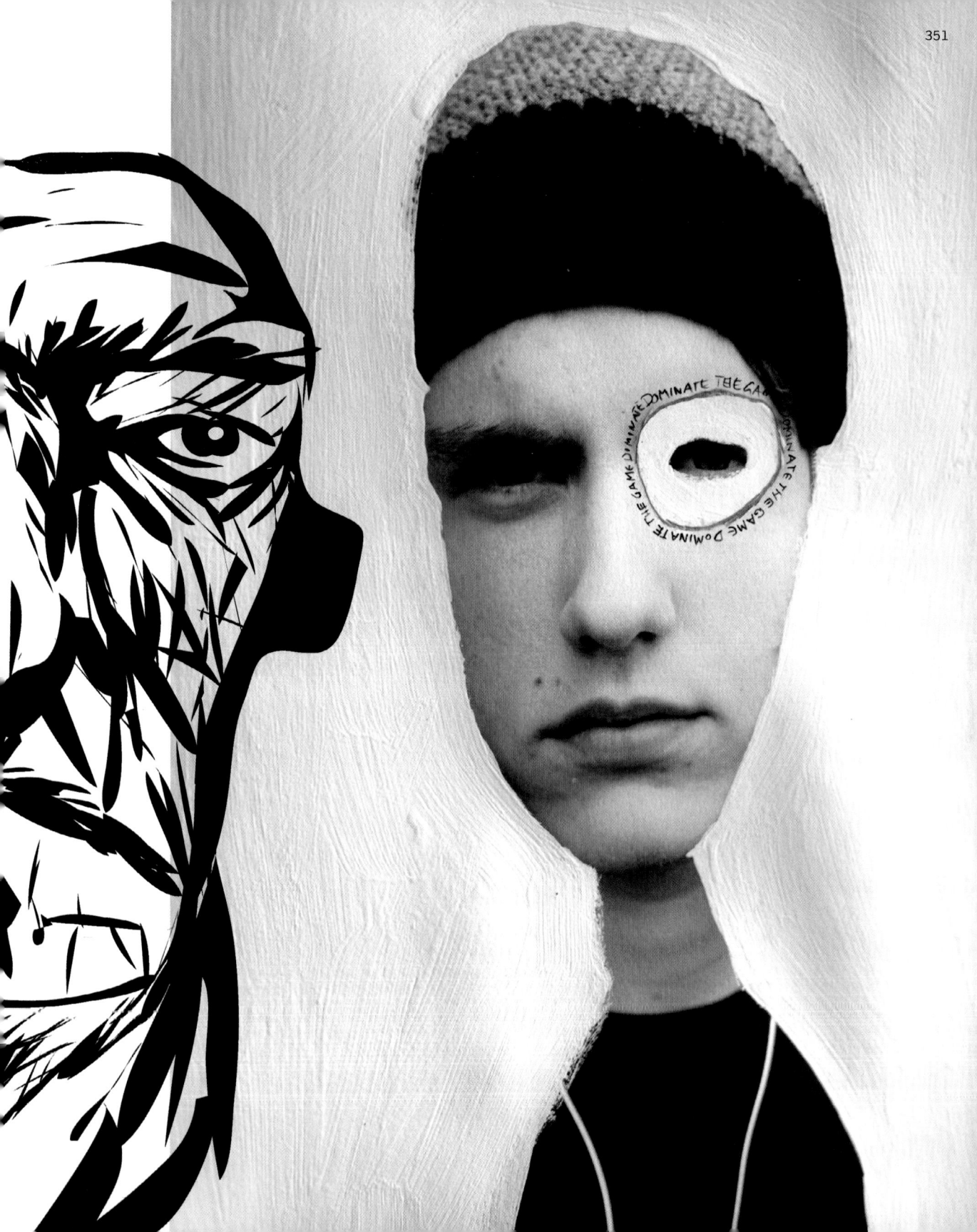

フォークが新宿さ

DESPUÉS DE UN DIÁLOGO CO
EL "DEMONIO" Y DE REPETIDAS
BLASFEMIAS O INJURIAS, LLEG
EL MOMENTO DEL SACRIFICIO.

¡HUUGGH!

TARO

50 ●

UM
FLAT
RATE
AFTER
4 P.M.

NO NOT DIGITAL
I AM USING A FILM CAMERA FOR MY WORK!

IN THAILAND SIND DIE
ELEFANTEN ARBEITSLOS
BULLDOZER ZIEHEN DAS HOLZ

WIR SITZEN IN FLACHEN
SITZGRUPPEN IN EXOTISCH
BARS. ESSEN PAD THAI UND
TRINKEN DIÄT COLA

OHNE ARBEIT BIST
DU FREMD

IN DER FREMDE
ARBEITEST DU NICHT...

JEDEN MORGEN
FLIEGT VOR
MEINEM FENSTER
EIN KOLIBRI

LOOK A
CHAR
SOME
ARE R

344

TINKA

JOHN WU

SKLAM

AFTER NINE MONTHS OF
EMPLOYMENT I OPENED
MY OWN OFFICE
WHEN I AM 40
I'LL GO TO EUROPE
RETIRE FROM WORK STUDY
DESIGN AND DRIVE
A BMW

MEXICAN WRESTLING

I DRIVE A MONSTER TRUCK THE GIRLS ARE PRETTY HERE!

RODMAN IS COOL AS SHIT

SAME SAME BUT DIFFERENT!

YOU NEED A BIGGER CAR

STANDARD IS GOING DOWN AND BUILDINGS ARE GOING UP THE INTERNATIONAL FINANCE CENTER IS THE HIGHEST IN TOWN!

IS THIS ASIA ?
IS THIS EUROPE ?
DOES ANYBODY CARE ?

IT'S A MONEY CAT
IT KNOCKS FOR MONEY

I SELL THIS TO FRIENDS

EVERYTHING CHANGES
THE HEAVY RED POST BOXES
CHANGED INTO THE UGLY
GREEN ONES EVEN THE
ROAD SIGNS CHANGED

YOU NEED A BIGGER CAR

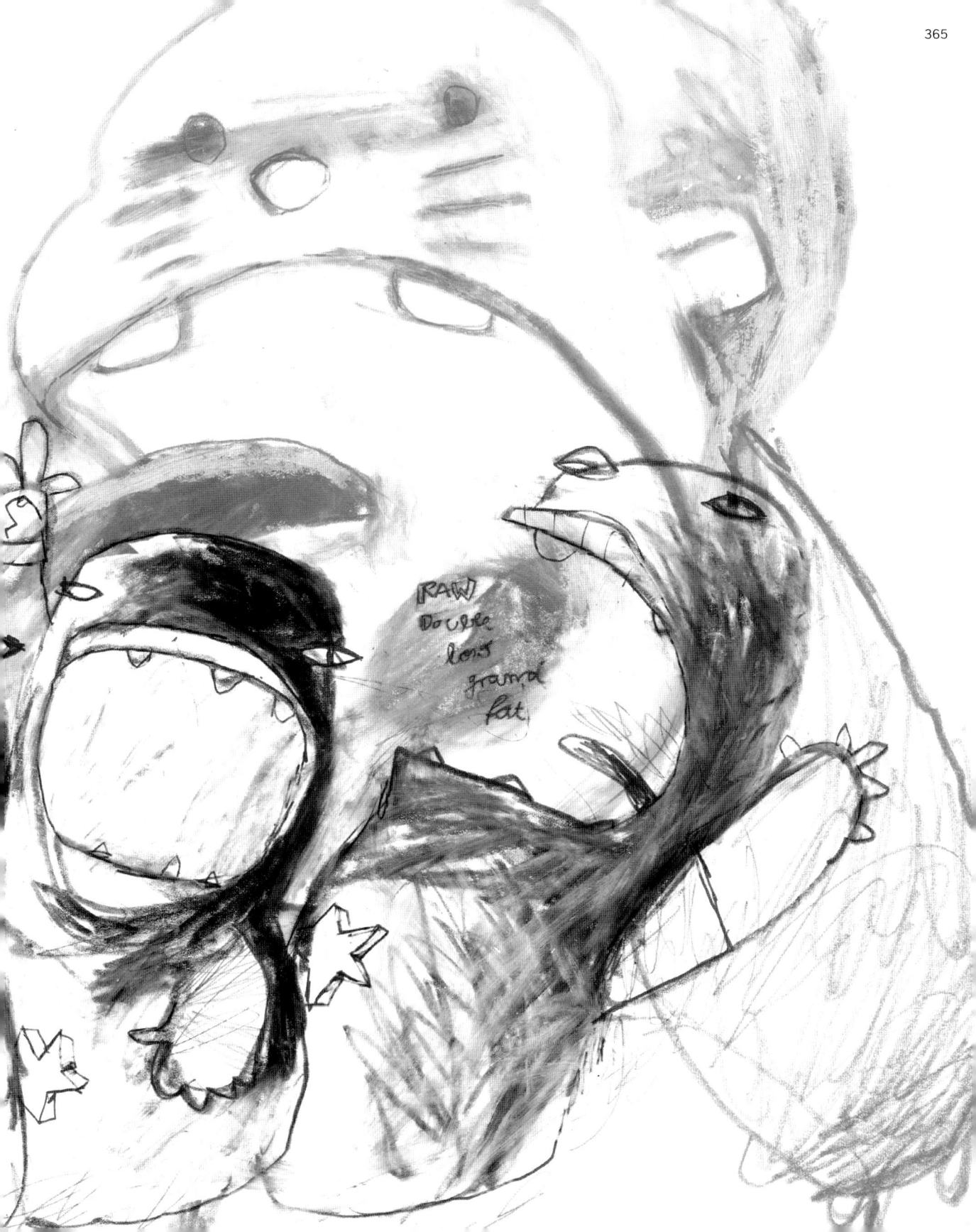

CHEZ TARO
IN TOKYO

stay

leave

BASTARD
FONTS

BLACK ROSE
COPY
CROSS
CUCARACHA
DEADMAN
DECOMIC OBLIQUE
DIAMOND
DOS.DE.TRES
FERTIGBAUHAUS
FILOU
FOOPER
FRAKTENDON
FRAKZIDENZ
GLOSSY
GRINGO
HERMAPHRODITE
MOUNTAIN
MR. J. SMITH
MULTIGENIC
NEWSLETTER STENCIL
SHIVER
SHUTTLE
STICH ME
TELETRON
YAVEZ

COPY __THOMAS METTENDORF KARLSRUHE, GERMANY www.schmalfett.de

REGULAR,
ITALIC, BOLD
24/48 PT

Dubai is an eerie **place**, **steaming** with the *superfluous*, trying to evolve into a **megapolis** while at the *core of its voice*

16 PT

abcdefghijklmnopqrsßtuvwxyz ABCDEFGHIJKLMNOPQR STUVWXYZ 1234567890 !?;–"«*áçøöåûñ/&€$)%§@ *abcdef ghijklmnopqrsßtuvwxyz ABCDEFGHIJKLMNOPQRSTUVWXYZ 1234567890* **abcdefghijklmnopqrsßtuvwxyz ABCDEFGHIJ KLMNOPQRSTUVWXYZ 1234567890**

9 PT

Growing up here was hard, I was viewed as a pretty young thing without a mind of my own – I was nearly deported for having sex with my then-boyfriend in a car, I went to jail for a day for smoking in a shopping mall (!), Arabs would pull up on the side of the road where I would be waiting for a bus and proposition me, **it was a sick,** twisted society that denied one's rights to one's own *sexuality* and yet tried to *"cash in"* on your womanhood as well. Also, Dubai was just plain boring in those days.
Dubai.. well.. its steaming away and I pass my days in the glass cage of a glossy ad agency and return home in the evenings to a villa I share with an unemployed Siberian couple, a German banker, an Englishman and two smelly cats.
During the day I am often logged onto MSN messenger where I keep in touch with friends and family splattered all over the globe including Alaska, Lebanon, Indonesia, Slovenia, Sweden, France, Nigeria and Spain. Bombay, which is, I believe, the physical embodiment of the space you might be trying to define that has consumed the people of our planet. Bombay is a seething mess of confused people searching for their identities in the face of globalisation and Western pop culture.
now I'm off to smoke myself sick.. my little friends with filters..

REGULAR,
ITALIC, BOLD
24/48 PT

it is a *village.* *Having grown* up here my **teenage thoughts** revolved around *escaping* on a cargo ship to

16 PT

abcdefghijklmnopqrsßtuvwxyz ABCDEFGHIJKLMNOPQR STUVWXYZ 1234567890 !?;–"«*áçøöåûñ/&€$)%§@ *abcde fghijklmnopqrsßtuvwxyz ABCDEFGHIJKLMNOPQRSTUVW XYZ 1234567890* **abcdefghijklmnopqrsßtuvwxyz ABCDEF GHIJKLMNOPQRSTUVWXYZ 1234567890**

REGULAR,
ITALIC, BOLD
24/48 PT

South America or perhaps stealing **money** to buy myself a *plane ticket* out of this "dead space"

16 PT

abcdefghijklmnopqrsßtuvwxyz ABCDEFGHIJKLMNOP QRSTUVWXYZ 1234567890 !?;–"«*áçøöåûñ/&€$)%§@ *abcdefghijklmnopqrsßtuvwxyz ABCDEFGHIJKLMNOPQ RSTUVWXYZ 1234567890* **abcdefghijklmnopqrsßtu vwxyz ABCDEFGHIJKLMNOPQRSTUVWXYZ 12357890**

9 PT

where the world's money hungry crawl. I used to image all the people here as "plastic people" and I imagined them melting in the sun. Dubai is a badly-planned, poorly envisioned attempt at *modernising* the Gulf's most important port.
On the outside everything looks manicured and neat,and on the inside its a hot-bed of *corruption, politics, racism, monopoly* and **power.**

GRINGO SANS/SLAB/TUSCAN _PETER BRUGGER KARLSRUHE, GERMANY

SANS
LIGHT
MEDIUM NARROW
BOLD WIDE
24/48 PT

I am an Indian born in Dubai, U.A.E, schooled in England, worked in Rome and India and **now** in the Gulf,

SLAB
LIGHT NARROW
BOLD NARROW
MEDIUM WIDE
24/48 PT

I have English and French blood, do not **speak my native language, but can speak** Arabic, French and Spanish.

TUSCAN
LIGHT
MEDIUM NARROW
BOLD WIDE
24/48 PT

I cook excellent Thai curry, travel the world, wear Gucci sandals and **Banana Republic t-shirts, eat McDonalds**

GRINGO SANS
FAMILY
16 PT

Light LightNarrow LightWide
Medium MediumNarrow MediumWide
Bold BoldNarrow BoldWide

SANS /
SLAB /
TUSCAN
MEDIUM WIDE /
GRINGO
DINGBATS
16 PT

abcdefghijklmnopqrsßtuvwxyz ABCDEFGHIJKLMNOPQ RSTUVWXYZ 1234567890 !?;«*áçøöåûñ/&€$]%§@ abc defghijklmnopqrsßtuvwxyz ABCDEFGHIJKLMNOPQRS TUVWXYZ 1234567890 abcdefghijklmnopqrsßtuvw xyz ABCDEFGHIJKLMNOPQRSTUVWXYZ 1234567890

SLAB
LIGHT
MEDIUM
BOLD
BOLD WIDE
9 PT

and buy egyptian antiquities. **I am a graffiti artist/writer and painter,** I studied animation film design, and I've worked as a swimming pool lifeguard, **a face painter at a children's fair, a t-shirt designer, a secretary, an illustrator, a stilt-walker in a circus, a film director, a television producer,** and am currently an **art director** at a top international advertising agency.

DIAMOND _LARS HARMSEN, HENRI ROUSSIER KARLSRUHE, GERMANY / VALENCE, FRANCE

LIGHT
REGULAR
BOLD
20/40 PT

kennst du **mucha lucha**
von cartoon network? **putamadre, no?**
saludos desde mexico, sandrita.

12 PT

abcdefghijklmnopqrstuvwxyz ABCDEFGHIJKLMNOPQRSTUV
WXYZ 1234567890 !?;-"áçöåû/&€$]%§@ abcdefghijklmnopqrst
uvwxyz ABCDEFGHIJKLMNOPQRSTUVWXYZ 1234567890 **abc**
defghijklmnopqrstuvwxyz ABCDEFGHIJKLMNOPQRSTUV
WXYZ 234567890

7 PT

thats sounds great. i might not be in tokyo 20th-22nd. but my wife Hina is around the gallery, so i think
she can meet you. maybe 23rd will be good for me. my gallery will have an **exhibition** at that time.
please call me or email me when you **come to tokyo.**

CROSS _LARS HARMSEN KARLSRUHE, GERMANY

TEN, TWENTY,
THIRTY, FOURTY,
SIXTY, ULTRA
32/64 PT

(My father) is an **architect,**
and so I grew up reading about
Mies, **Le Corbusier** and Rem Koolhaas

20 PT

abcdefghijklmnopqrsßtuvwxyz ABCDEFGHIJKLMNOPQRSTU
VWXYZ 1234567890 !?;-"«*áçøöåûñ/&€$)%§⌐ abcdefghijk
lmnopqrsßtuvwxyz ABCDEFGHIJKLMNOPQRSTUVWXYZ 123456
7890 abcdefghijklmnopqrsßtuvwxyz ABCDEFGHIJKLMNOPQ
RSTUVWXYZ 1234567890 abcdefghijklmnopqrsßtuvwxyz
ABCDEFGHIJKLMNOPQRSTUVWXYZ 1234567890 abcdefghijk
lmnopqrsßtuvwxyz ABCDEFGHIJKLMNOPQRSTUVWXYZ 123
4567890 abcdefghijklmnopqrsßtuvwxyz ABCDEFGHIJ
KLMNOPQRSTUVWXYZ 1234567890

HERMAPHRODITE _ STEFAN CLAUDIUS   ESSEN, GERMANY   www.cape-arcona.com

REGULAR
ITALIC
28/56 PT

Thanks for your **ANSWERS.**
How about THURSDAY, 13:00?
Let me know.

16 PT

abcdefghijklmnopqrsßtuvwxyz ABCDEFGHIJKLMNOPQRSTUVWXYZ
1234567890 !?;–"«*áçøöåûñ/&€$) %§@ *abcdefghijklmnopqrsßtuvwxyz*
ABCDEFGHIJKLMNOPQRSTUVWXYZ 1234567890

9 PT

My schedule of our journey is. From sunday 4rd through next sunday we will be at Barcelona, except 6th and 7th because we
are going to Bilbao. We will be in Italy from the 12th through 19th, 3 days in Rome, after Venice and probably Milan. *We return
to BCN for 2 days and we will fly to Amsterdam only for two days, we'll come back to BCN and take a flight to London for also
only two days. We will arrive on the 25th to Barcelona to take a flight back home the day after 26th.* Please let me know where
do you think you can meet me, of course i'd rather meet you in Barcelona as it will be the place that i will be staying the longer

CUCARACHA _ RENÉ VERKAART   MAASTRICHT, THE NETHERLANDS   www.characters.nl

FONT
24/36/48 PT

Actually I write u **because** I âm
doing a PUBLIC SPACE intervention Project
STREET ART here, in Mexico

WIXA
24 PT

abcdefghijklmnopqrstuvwxyz
ABCDEFGHIJKLMNOPQRSTUVW
XYZ 1234567890 ÄÖÜÄÄÖÜ

ICONS
24 PT

MOUNTAIN _DAN REYNOLDS OFFENBACH/FFM, GERMANY www.typeoff.de

REGULAR
ITALIC
SMALL CAPS
SC ITALIC
26/52 PT

The **Project** was generated last june in BUENOS AIRES *AND NOW I HAVE DEVELOPED THE SITE OF IT, THE IDEA OF*

14 PT

abcdefghijklmnopqrsßtuvwxyz ABCDEFGHIJKLMNOPQRSTUVWXYZ 12345 67890 !?;–"«*áçøöåûñ/€\$)%§@ *abcdefghijklmnopqrsßtuvwxyz ABCDEFG HIJKLMNOPQRSTUVWXYZ 1234567890* ABCDEFGHIJKLMNOPQRSSSTUVWXYZ 1234567890 *ABCDEFGHIJKLMNOPQRSTUVWXYZ 1234567890*

NEWSLETTER STENCIL _INGO KREPINSKY BREMEN/HAMBURG, GERMANY www.typonauten.de

24/48 PT

To see how **possible** is to find a SPACE in your site to describe my PROJECT. (might b an article?)

16 PT

abcdefghijklmnopqrsßtuvwxyz ABCDEFGHIJKLMNOPQRSTUV WXYZ 1234567890 !?.–"«*áç øöåûñ/€\$)%§@

SHUTTLE _HEINRICH LISCHKA KÖTHEN, GERMANY www.fontboutique.de

NORMAL
SOFT
3D
3D FILL
3D SHADOW
24 PT

I AM VERY RELATED WITH ALL THE UNDER AND UPPER GROUND MOVEMENT, **FROM WRITERS, PHOTOGRAPHERS, ARTISTS,** ILLUSTRATORS, MUSICIANS, ETC.

16 PT

ABCDEFGHIJKLMNOPQRSSSTUVWIYZ ABCDEFGHIJKLMNOPQRSTUVWXYZ 1234567890 !?;–"«*ÁÇØÖÅÛÑ/&€\$)%§@ ABCDEFGHIJKLMNOPQRSTUVWXYZ 1234567890 ABCDEFGHIJ KLMNOPQRSTUVWXYZ 1234567890 ABCDEFGHIJKLMNOPQRSTUVWXYZ 12345678 90 ABCDEFGHIJKLMNOPQRSTUVWXYZ 1234567890

FOOPER _LARS HARMSEN, MATTHIAS KANTEREIT KARLSRUHE, GERMANY

24 PT

the **way** like the **page** developing and the design of it (into the designerâs perspective)

16 PT

abcdefghijklmnopqrsßtuvwxyz ABCDEFGHIJKLMNOPQRS
TUVWXYZ 1234567890 !?;-"«*áçöåûñ/ &€$)%§@

9 PT

Malheureusement, je ne sais pas encore si je vais être là ou non, car c'est mon mois de
réserve et je ne saurai que la veille ou le jour même où j'irais. Mais je laisse de toute façon
une paire de clefs à un ami au cas ou je ne serais pas là.
Il me faudrait, s'il te plait vos noms et âges à tous les trois car je vis dans un immeuble
qui appartient à ma compagnie et je dois les prévenir de toute visite. (non non je n'habite
pas dans une prison). Vous serez notés comme étant mes cousins.

SHIVER _CHRISTOPH RANKERS FREIBURG, GERMANY

24 PT

At times you'll find **members** of the **Creative** Team skateboarding around the office with fire extinguishers

16 PT

abcdefghijklmnopqrsßtuvwxyz ABCDEFGHIJKLMNOPQR
STUVWXYZ 1234567890 !?;-"«*áçöåûñ/&$)%§@

FRAKTENDON _LARS HARMSEN, BORIS KAHL KARLSRUHE, GERMANY

24 PT

After that we could go to a extremely NEO FOLK dance hall, a very popular place called Rodeo Revillagigedo

16 PT

abcdefghijklmnopqrsßtuvwxyz ABCDEFGHIJKLMNOPQRS
TUVWXYZ 1234567890 !?;-"«*áçöåûñ/&$)%§@

BLACK ROSE _ESCOBAS
MÉXICO CITY, MEXICO   www.escobas.com.mx

28/42/56 PT

taping *iPods* to the ceiling, playing chess, WEARING lettuce leaf „crowns , nice casual surrounding

16 PT

abcdefghijklmnopqrsßtuvwxyz ABCDEFGHIJKLMNOPQR STUVWXYZ 1234567890 !?;–"«*áçøöåûñ/&¤$)%§@

DEADMAN _CHRISTOPH SEILER
KARLSRUHE, GERMANY

DEADman REGULAR /
DEADman BLOTTING /
DEADman SQUIRTING
30/60 pt

within which we churn out some seriously award-winning work. What is it like to be a designer in

16 PT

abcdefghijklmnopqrsßtuvwxyz ABCDEFGHIJKLMNOPQRSTUVWXYZ 1234567890 !?; "«*aöû/&$)%§@ . . . . .

FILOU _BORIS KAHL
KARLSRUHE, GERMANY

REGULAR
MEDIUM
EXTRA
26/48 PT

evolving *Feeling* of Confusion, false NOTIONS of Comfort AND Mediocrity mixed with a need to move on

16 PT

abcdefghijklmnopqrsßtuvwxyz ABCDEFGHIJKLMNOPQ RSTUVWXYZ 1234567890 !?;–"*áöû/&$)%§@ ABCDEFG HIJKLMNOPQRSTUVWXYZ ABCDEFGHIJKLM NOPQRSTUVWXYZ

FRAKZIDENZ _SIRKKA HAMMER PFORZHEIM, GERMANY

MINI
30/45/60 PT

Es ist schon sehr spannend zu sehen wie ein junger Nigerianer zum ersten Mal McDonalds betritt

BOLD
20 PT

abcdefghijklmnopqrsßtuvwxyz ABCDEFGHIJKLMNOPQR STUVWXYZ 1234567890 !?;-

MINI
11 PT

Without much doubt we scrape up against cultural understandings and limits with our extremly pacifistic and nobel project in one of the most dirty cities on the planet. We do not only eat dirt as a side scoope, but dodge cars for fun, money and teatch the drivers to use there sidemirrows or take them ride off anyways.........
Ciclos still try to keep a company stile in two blue colors, so we might not look quite as bastards bad ass as the ny messenger style book.

STICH ME_MARTINA HARTMANN COLOGNE, GERMANY

STICH ME
STICH DINGS
20/40/90 PT

and enjoying seeing that its not only mexico df that suffers from absolute crazy traffic and finding streets impossible.

STICH ME
STICH DINGS
14 PT

abcdefghijklmnopqrsßtuvwxyz ABCDEFGHIJKLMNOPQRS TUVWXYZ 1234567890 !?;-*áçöäûñ/&$)½@

STICH ME
9 PT

Je vis avec 2 flatmates, elles t ouvrirons. Deplus un de mes copains a la clé donc il ny a pas de problèmes. Je vous propose de prendre un taxi à votre arrivée à l aeroport (je n ai pas encore de voiture) j habite à 10 minutes. Et je vous attendrais au bas de mon immeuble. Voici mon adresse

DECOMIC OBLIQUE _ PAUL HOPPE, BORIS KAHL   NEW YORK, USA / KARLSRUHE, GERMANY   www.paulhoppe.de

27/54 PT

I have made several FILMS on the theme of the Self and the Other and an ongoing PHOTOGRAPHY project

16 PT

*abcdefghijklmnopqrssstuvwxyz ABCDEFGHIJKLMNOPQRSTUVWXYZ 1234567890 !?;– "«*áçôåûñ|&€$)%@*

GLOSSY _ SANDRA HOFACKER   ZÜRICH, SWITZERLAND   www.sware-design.de

24/36 PT

I have many stories, thoughts, feelings, paranoias and curry recipes.

14 PT

abcdefghijklmnopqrstuvwxyz ABCDEFGHIJKL MNOPQRSTUVWXYZ 1234567890?!./8, %$$$@

FERTIGBAUHAUS _ DAVID HUBNER   LINZ, AUSTRIA   www.formlos.net

24 PT

musek have been attempting to understand identities by many of my own projects

16 PT

abcdefghijklmnopqrstuvwxyz .@

MR. J. SMITH _L. HARMSEN, U. WEISS, B. KAHL, N. RENGER KARLSRUHE, GERMANY

HEAD, EYES,
NOSE, MOUTH
80/40 PT

WANTED
24 PT

WANTED
24 PT

abcdefghijklmnopqrsßtuvwxyz ABCDEFGHIJKLMNO
PQRSTUVWXYZ 1234567890 !?;–"*áçöaûñ/&€$)%@

TELETRON _MICHEL M. MÜNSTER, GERMANY www.michelm.org

COPY HIGH,
COPY LOW,
MEDIA HIGH,
MEDIA LOW
16 PT

16 PT

DOS.DE.TRES __ESCOBAS__ MÉXICO CITY, MEXICO   www.escobas.com.mx

72/36/24 PT

YAVEZ __ESCOBAS__ MÉXICO CITY, MEXICO   www.escobas.com.mx

34/68 PT

MULTIGENIC __BORIS KAHL__ KARLSRUHE, GERMANY

24/36 PT

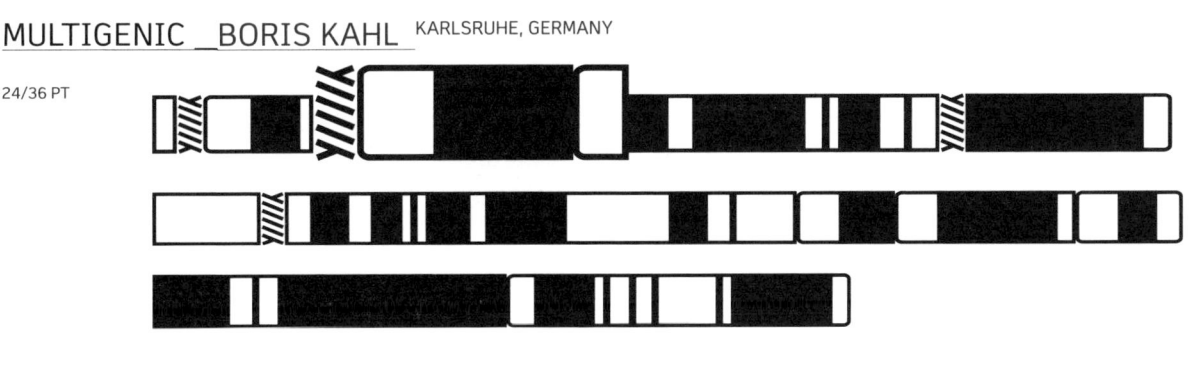

14 PT

BASTARD
INDEX

INTERVIEW
AUTHORS
CREDITS

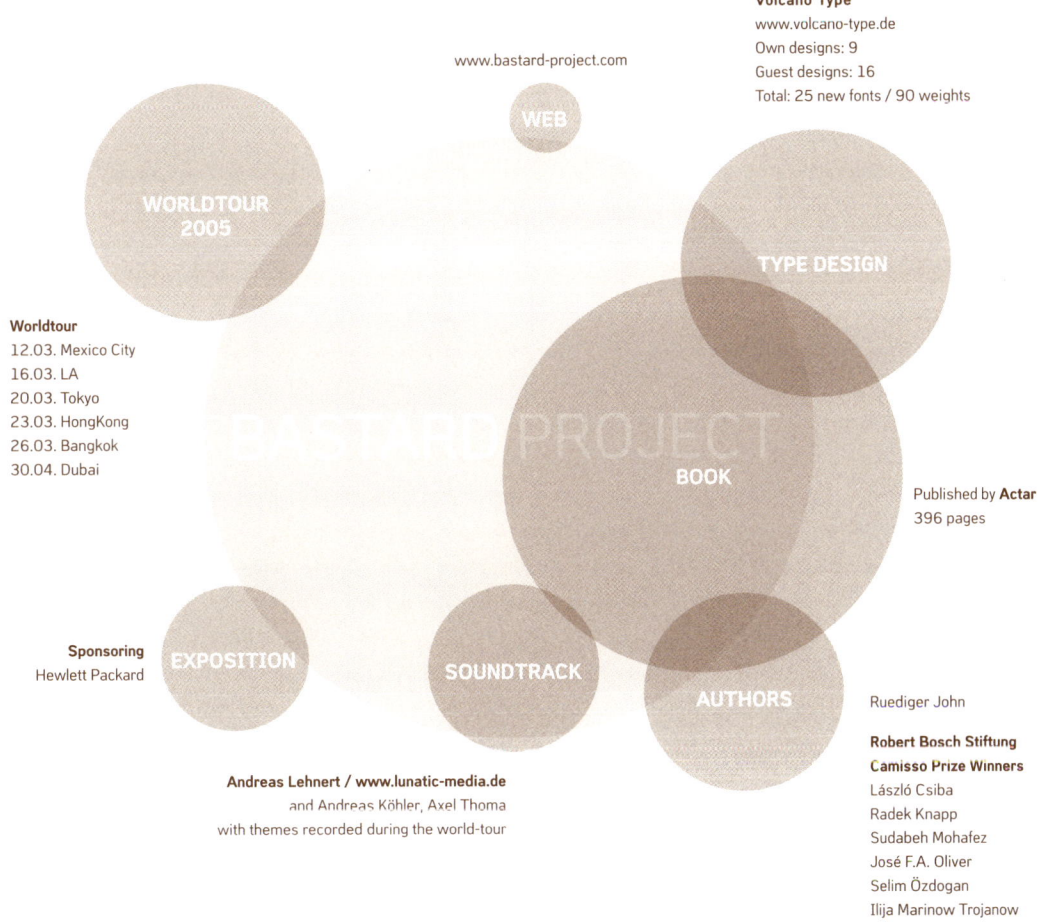

Volcano Type
www.volcano-type.de
Own designs: 9
Guest designs: 16
Total: 25 new fonts / 90 weights

www.bastard-project.com

WEB

WORLDTOUR
2005

TYPE DESIGN

Worldtour
12.03. Mexico City
16.03. LA
20.03. Tokyo
23.03. HongKong
26.03. Bangkok
30.04. Dubai

BOOK

Published by **Actar**
396 pages

Sponsoring
Hewlett Packard

EXPOSITION

SOUNDTRACK

AUTHORS

Ruediger John

Robert Bosch Stiftung
Camisso Prize Winners
László Csiba
Radek Knapp
Sudabeh Mohafez
José F.A. Oliver
Selim Özdogan
Ilija Marinow Trojanow

Andreas Lehnert / www.lunatic-media.de
and Andreas Köhler, Axel Thoma
with themes recorded during the world-tour

IT DOESN'T END WITH THIS BOOK

Sigrid Frank-Eßlinger: *Three of you, André, Christian and Lars, traveled around the world to make this book: the BASTARD book. You started in Frankfurt and traveled to Mexico City, Los Angeles, Tokyo, Hong Kong, Bangkok, Dubai and back. Why 21 days? And why these cities?*

Christian Ernst: Usually, we all do commercial work to earn a living, and that's why we decided to devote 21 days to a topic of our choice. Not with the goal to complete something in particular, but rather simply with the desire to search for something. 21 days without an assignment, without the family. Artist for 21 days! It may not sound like a long time, but it really is. For me, it was a luxury. That's when it occurred to us that we could travel around the world. But not because we wanted to visit these cities in particular. There are at least 20 other cities that are just as important to me.

Lars Harmsen: The BASTARD project is a follow-up to the VERSUS book, which Uli, Christian and I collaborated on. It's an extension of our font and typography work. We've started having a greater interest in bastarding fonts.

André Rösler: The important thing is that we never said: Let's take a trip and write a book about it. Lars first came up with the idea to BASTARD, and then we started thinking about how we could artistically realize the project.

Christian Ernst: We thought things over for three weeks, and then we planned the trip.

Ulrich Weiß: Part of the concept was that we'd only be able to stay on the surface of things this way. But facades are extremely honest and good representations of society.

André Rösler: Yes, and speed is also an extremely important aspect, which the BASTARD concept addresses. Of course, speed is normal in our world, but it hasn't been as global, as fast and as forceful in the past as it is today. Since we traveled to so many cities within only three weeks, we quasi forced speed upon our very own bodies. And we wanted to see just how our perception of things would change when we were subjected to constant activity, change and jetlag. That was our experiment.

Sigrid Frank-Eßlinger: *In other words, the fact that you only had 21 days to travel around the world didn't really posit a problem, because time and speed were a part of the concept?*

Christian Ernst: I constantly had the feeling that I wasn't able to take in as much as I wanted to; everything just moved too fast. My perceptions of the individual cities became blurred and constantly shifted. And yet, I never got the feeling that if I'd stayed two or three more days in one place, it would have changed anything. We would hardly make it to the next flight, and there was the next city pushing us on.

Lars Harmsen: 21 days to go around the world mirrors what the Internet is all about. You sit down in front of your computer, send an e-mail clear across the globe and a few minutes later you've already got a reply. We moved with the same speed and subjected ourselves to the very same forces which urge on globalization.

Ulrich Weiß: High speeds and networks were two themes you explored on this trip. The effect it had on your bodies was a part of the experiment. You didn't know beforehand if it would really work, if you would get something out of the experience, if you would actually make it. I mean there was always the possibility that you'd keel over after 12 days.

André Rösler: We visited the cities as if we were flipping through foreign design books, or web pages. You don't know who the designer is, where he or she lives, what he or she does. But that isn't what's essential right then and there, because you're looking directly at what the designer is doing.

Christian Ernst: We couldn't predict in advance what would happen. During the trip, we actually just collected material, and it was first later that we really started working. We were absolutely drained afterward, but we had photographs, tape recordings and drawings to take home with us. And lots of memories. We met people on our journey, talked with them at length and got to know them. And just as we had taken them into our hearts, we had to go. I'll never forget Mexico City, where André and Lars talked with ten typographers for hours about typography and drawing. That wasn't an experience you could call superficial! If it were, then we would've been nothing more that voyeurs running through one city after another.

André Rösler: Yes, that's right, but, at the same time, we never did anything as a kind of study.

Christian Ernst: No, we didn't want to travel around feeling like we were doing research. Maybe, in an artistic vein, but, basically, we just wanted to perceive things.

André Rösler: Yes, perceive is a better word.

Sigrid Frank-Eßlinger: You wanted to feel and perceive globalization. And what was it like? What did you feel? What did you experience?

Christian Ernst: I can't say what the best or most important experiences were. Our work and the book are meant to show that process. We were in motion, and we're still in motion.

Ulrich Weiß: The process doesn't just end; it doesn't end with this book.

Christian Ernst: (laughing) And in the end, there will be a twelve-volume BASTARD Encyclopedia. This is only volume one.

Lars Harmsen: Before we left on our trip, we contacted people we didn't know. And all of our encounters with them ended up being extremely intense, friendly and enjoyable. We never had the feeling that we were tourists. We felt that we belonged and were amongst colleagues. We met people whose brains tick like ours. And because of that, we always felt comfortable immediately, although we were in a foreign setting. That's something that made a big impression on me. I never felt like I was a tourist.

Christian Ernst: Yes, and it was also nice to feel that the people we met thought it was special to meet us, too. Globalization or no globalization. And the fact that it's possible to meet colleagues in Mexico City or Hong Kong without having some big contract deal in one's suitcase was also something that amazed me. I mean, they were taking time out of their busy lives for us.

André Rösler: What I won't forget is the way I perceived the individual cities. It's different when you set off from home to travel to one particular place than it is to fly from one foreign place to the next. It completely changes your way of perceiving things. When you visit four, five, or six cities in a row, you perceive them differently than you would if you were flying from your hometown directly to, say, Tokyo. It made me more sensitive to the cities and the people. I suddenly started making completely different comparisons. I asked myself how the people were in one place compared to another. And the effect of this: being able to make direct comparisons was something I had never thought of before. And by meeting with so many different designers, we also noticed with what full force globalization has hit this branch. Someone shows you a pocket book with Mexican ornamental art in Mexico, and then you discover the exact same book in Hong Kong and Tokyo at the design shops. That's when you notice that our brains think alike. That's globalization. That's bastarding. The same plastic figures, the same office interiors, the same hand bags. It was the same across-the-board, and this really surprised me.

Lars Harmsen: (smiling) Did you think everyone else was drawing stick figures in the sand with little pieces of wood and calling it design?

André Rösler: No, no, that's not what I mean. I'm just saying that their work could have been much more influenced by their cultural surroundings.

Christian Ernst: You could interpret that in a negative sense, of course: that everything is the same. But when you meet people you notice the diversity of cultures. Everyone is afraid of standardization. When everyone has the same design books does that mean young designers everywhere will use the same design? No – people are individual and influenced in different ways. They're simply different, and that was definitely a relief to discover!

Sigrid Frank-Eßlinger: Now you're back. Did the trip change you? Did it change your work? What have you gained from the experience?

André Rösler: After the trip, I thought a lot about what I do compared to all the people we met. And I'm impressed that everything we collected on the trip is really consistent: due to the fact that we shared the same experiences. Also the work we did at the very beginning. I was afraid that certain things would fall by the wayside, that they wouldn't fit into the context. But now, suddenly, everything has fallen into place. Probably, because the foundation of our work, design-wise, is the same.

Christian Ernst: I started out sorting through and choosing pictures from the masses of photos we had collected, trying to get an idea of what we'd done during the three weeks. First now, just like André, I've reached the point where I feel that our work has started coming together to create a whole. But other than that: my freelance work hasn't changed at all; it's completely separate from the BASTARD project. But having worked together with colleagues on this project has, of course, influenced me and changed me personally. It's been an extremely good feeling, to work in a team that is getting something put together. This wasn't something I was aware of right away; it became more and more obvious as time went by.

Lars Harmsen: I noticed just how small Karlsruhe is. And that traveling, going out into the world, is, for me, the only way that I can be content within the small cosmos I call my home. I have to bring the world to me, in order to feel gratified. If I were to live in a city like Hong Kong, I'd probably go to the desert, or go sit on top of a mountain. It was a real necessity for me to leave the small, safe little world in which I live. And our trip was totally able to achieve this.

As far as my work is concerned, it gave important impulses. I noticed that radical changes in my environment stimulate my development within graphic art and help me reach new levels of quality. This project definitely did that. Simply because I observed, worked, was involved in discussions and was a part of a team. And as a designer, I learned a lot. I've experienced new things and broadened my mind, and I'll be able to pass that on to my customers.

And it's nice that friendships have developed, and that some of us are now working on other projects with people we met. It's great that team work with so many different kinds of people can actually work. Up until now, I've never worked on an interdisciplinary project like this one before, which combines illustration, photography, typography and graphic design. It was an experiment, and at the beginning no one really knew if it would work. If we'd be able to put it all together and create one homogenous work. If it did work, that's not for us to judge. But as far as we're concerned, this project was a totally new and thrilling experience.

Ulrich Weiss, Christian Ernst, André Rösler, Lars Harmsen

EDITORS

CHRISTIAN ERNST
Photographer, born in Karlsruhe, Germany in 1965

Christian Ernst, inspired by his father, began taking pictures when he was twelve years old. After completing school, he worked for several advertising photographers in Germany, as assistant and partner. For the past ten years, he has been a freelance photographer working for companies all over Europe. Christian Ernst has been involved in many books on architecture and art. Through his work, he has come in contact with such artists as Lüpertz, Penk, Immendorf, Nietsch and Malakov, to name a few. He was involved in a book project, entitled VERSUS, which he collaborated on with Lars Harmsen and Ulrich Weiß. This book is a good example of the kind of work he has been engaged in for the past few years.

LARS HARMSEN
Graphic-designer, born in Hannover, Germany in 1964

Lars Harmsen spent the first four years of his life in Chicago. He then moved to Geneva with his parents for eight years, where he learned to speak French, and then moved to Karlsruhe. He completed his schooling at the French section at the European School. He first studied history and Germanics in Freiburg before beginning to study design at Basel, Boston, Saarbrücken and Pforzheim. He got his degree in graphic design, and in 1996 he founded MAGMA [Büro für Gestaltung] together with Ulrich Weiß. He is the co-founder of STARSHOT GmbH, a design company for sports products, now based in Munich. MAGMA created Type Foundry Volcano-Type.de and the internet forum Slanted.de. In the meantime, Slanted.de has become the most active German typography forum.

ANDRE RÖSLER
Illustrator, born in Lahr (Black Forest), Germany in 1970

André Rösler studied design at the *Fachhochschule für Gestaltung Pforzheim*, and after earning his degree in 1997 *Diplom-Designer(FH)* he worked there as an assistant. He is co-founder of *mal4 - Bürogemeinschaft für Gestaltung* in Karlsruhe, and has worked as a freelance illustrator and designer since 1996. In 1999, he became involved in making and directing animation films for *Anschi und Karl-Heinz*, a children's television program aired weekly. In 2003, André Rösler illustrated the picture book *Kannst du brüllen?* published by Peter Hammer Publishing house, and in 2005, a children's book entitled *Emil wird sieben*. The author of both books was Karin Koch. In 2004, Rösler was awarded the ADC-Preis (Art-Directors Club Deutschland) for his illustrations in a book entitled *Gutes Benehmen im Galopp*.

ULRICH WEISS
Graphic-designer, born in Pforzheim, Germany in 1966

Deeply rooted to his region of birth, Ulrich Weiß decided to study design at the art school in Pforzheim, where he met his future partner Lars Harmsen, and earned a degree as in graphic design (Diplom). Before founding MAGMA [Büro für Gestaltung] together with Mr. Harmsen, he worked for several years as creative director for J. G & Partner in Baden-Baden. Last year, Ulrich Weiß collaborated on a typography and photography book, entitled VERSUS, together with Lars Harmsen and Christian Ernst. The book was published by dgv Die Gestalten Verlag in Berlin.

AUTHORS / ROBERT BOSCH STIFTUNG

All the contributors to this book, except Ruediger John, who wrote the introduction, are recipients of the Adelbert-von-Chamisso-Prize which is awarded by the Robert Bosch Foundation. The prize honors books published in the German language by authors who come from non-German-speaking backgrounds. The prize has been presented since 1985. More information on the prize and the foundation can be found on the web: www.bosch-stiftung.de

LASZLO CSIBA
Born in Mosonmagyaróvár, Hungary in 1949

László Csiba moved to the DDR in 1968 and studied literature from 1988 to 1991 at the *Literaturinstitut Leipzig*. From 1978 to 1979, he translated several works of Hungarian prose and poetry. Since 1981, he has written various short literary works, short stories and poems in German. He has received many grants, including a grant from the *Kultusministerium des Landes Sachsen-Anhalt*, the *Künstlerhaus Wiepersdorf*, the *Art Stiftung Plaas*, Lindau am Bodensee and the *Kuratorium der Stiftung Kulturfonds*, Berlin. Csiba was awarded the *Adelbert-von-Chamisso-Förderpreis* in 1995; in 2000, a grant was awarded Mr. Csiba by the Robert-Bosch-Foundation for his radio play „Ich töte Mozart nicht".

SELECTED PUBLICATIONS
Gleichgewichtsstörung, stories, Tübingen, *1995*; **Durch das Flugloch der Bleistiftspitze**, poems, *1998*; **Das Lachen der Fische**, poems, *2003*; **ich liebe zu frühstücken**, poems, *2004*

RADEK KNAPP
Born in Warsaw, Poland in 1964

Radek Knapp grew up with his grandparents in the Polish countryside. In 1976, he moved to Vienna to live with his mother. There, he began to study philosophy and write stories, while working various odd jobs to get by. In 1992, Mr. Knapp was awarded the *Nachwuchsstipendium für Literatur* awarded by the *Bundesministerium für Unterricht und Kunst*. In 1993, he won the *Würdigungspreis* awarded by the city of Vienna, and in 1999/2000 he received a *Projektstipendium für Literatur* awarded by the BKA. In 1994, he received the *Aspekte-Literaturpreis* for his pastoral-grotesque tales, entitled Franio, a collection of stories set in the Polish countryside. In 2001, Mr. Knapp was awarded the *Adelbert-von-Chamisso-Förderpreis*.

SELECTED PUBLICATIONS
Ein Bericht, stories, *1989*; **Franio**, stories, *1996*; **Herrn Kukas Empfehlungen**, novel, *1999*; **Papiertiger, Eine Geschichte in fünf Episoden**, *2003*; **Gebrauchsanweisung für Polen**, *2005*

SUDABEH MOHAFEZ
Born in Teheran, Iran in 1963

Since 1979, Sudabeh Mohafez has been based in Berlin. She has studied music, English literature and pedagogy, and has been a part of several non-governmental organizations doing work in migration and violence prevention issues. She now lives and works as a freelance author in Germany and Portugal. For the novel *Gespräch in Meeresnähe*, Mohafez received a grant awarded by the *Berliner Senatsverwaltung für Wissenschaft, Forschung und Kultur*, and in 2006, she received the *Adelbert-von-Chamisso-Förderpreis* for her collection of stories entitled *Wüstenhimmel, Sternenland*.

SELECTED PUBLICATIONS
Wüstenhimmel, Sternenland, stories *2004*; **Gespräch in Meeresnähe**, novel *2005*; **Gästezimmer**, novel included in: Entwürfe Nr. 43, 2005
www.sudabehmohafez.de

JOSÉ F.A. OLIVER
Born in Hausach (the Black Forest), Germany in 1961

José F.A. Oliver is the child of Andalusian working migrants. He studied Romance languages, Germanics and philosophy at the University Freiburg, and began writing both poetry and short prose texts in German, as well as Spanish at a very early age. From 1988 to 1997, he was awarded several grants. In 1997, he was awarded the *Adelbert-von-Chamisso-Preis* for all of his literary work to date. In 2001, Oliver was *Stadtschreiber* (poeta laureatus) for the city of Dresden, and in 2004, he was the *Stadtschreiber* for Cairo, participating in the midad-project which was organized by the Goethe-Institute. In 2002, he was guest professor and writer-in-residence at the Massachusetts Institute of Technology in Cambridge, USA.

SELECTED PUBLICATIONS
Weil ich dieses Land liebe, poems, *1991;* **Austernfischer Marinero Vogelfrau**, *1997*; **Fernlautmetz,** poems, *2000*; **nachtrandspuren**, poems, *2002*; **finnischer wintervorrat**, poems, *2005*.
www.suhrkamp.de

SELIM ÖZDOGAN
Born in Cologne, Germany in 1971

Selim Özdogan is a German author with Turkish roots. He grew up speaking both Turkish and German in Cologne. After earning his Abitur, he studied ethnology, English literature and philosophy without earning a degree. Mr. Özdogan works as a newspaper and magazine writer. His first novel was published in 1995. In 1996, Özdogan was awarded the *Förderpreis des Landes Nordrhein-Westfalen* in the category Young Artist/Poet/Author. In 1999, he received the *Adelbert-von-Chamisso-Förderpreis* awarded by the Robert-Bosch-Foundation.

SELECTED PUBLICATIONS
Es ist so einsam im Sattel, seit das Pferd tot ist, novel *1995*; **Ein gutes Leben ist die beste Rache**, stories *1998*; **Ein Spiel, das die Götter sich leisten**, *2002*; **Trinkgeld vom Schicksal**, *2003*; **Die Tochter des Schmieds**, novel *2005*
www.selimoezdogan.de

ILIJA MARINOW TROJANOW
Born in Sofia, Bulgaria in 1965

Ilija Trojanow was granted political asylum in Germany in 1971 after his family fled to Italy through Yugoslavia. From 1972, he lived in Kenya for several years, attending a local German school. After earning his *Abitur*, he studied law and ethnology in Munich and began taking journalistic assignments. In 1998, he moved to Bombay, India and has since then worked mainly as a journalist and translator in that city. In addition to numerous grants, Trojanow has been honored with many prizes, amongst them the *Bertelsmann-Literaturpreis* in 1995, the *Literaturpreis der Stadt Marburg* in 1996, the *Viktor-von-Scheffel-Preis* in 1997, and the *Adelbert-von-Chamisso-Preis* in 2000.

SELECTED PUBLICATIONS
Die Welt ist groß und Rettung lauert überall, novel, *1999*; **Der Sadhu an der Teufelswand**, eye-witness accounts, *2002*; **An den inneren Ufern Indiens**, a travel account, *2003*; **Zu den heiligen Quellen des Islam**, a pilgrimage, *2004*

RUEDIGER JOHN
Artist, Austrian, born in Germany in 1971

Ruediger John creates situative, installative, interventionistic, research- and publication-oriented works and exhibitions, as well as definitoric and practical works on Artistic Research and Systemic Art. He has been invited to participate in numerous events, exhibitions and panel discussions.
Since 1995, he also works artistically as Critical Aesthetic Coach and Consultant. Since 2000, he has held several teaching positions. He is the founder of the *Gesellschaft für kritische Ästhetik* (Society of Critical Aesthetics).

PUBLICATIONS:
Erweiterte Erkenntnisfähigkeit durch kulturelle Kontextualisierung, *2005*; **Objekt Subjekt Prädikat**, *2005*; **TRANSFER: Kunst Wirtschaft Wissenschaft**, *2003*; **Die Akademie ist keine Akademie**, *1999*; **Scrapbook 1995-1998**, *1998*; **short essays and narrative fragments**, *1997*; **Central Park 1 AM**, *1994*; **book - an object oriented definition of an infrastructure**, *1991*
www.artrelated.net/ruediger__john

EVERY DAY (Pages 68-98) / **Sudabeh Mohafez**

Page 68 there are still people who go to work every day the world just didn't stop turning they take the subway today like every day and I can't stop myself from asking the same question what everyday can mean starting now / the roses **70** I left them / some people dream in the morning and I can't help but wonder **72** why the world doesn't just stop damn it / the bouquet in the hotel sink water: for when it's time **74** it's time now **76** and I ask myself how I'll be able to reach you when the earth keeps on spinning like this / those roses can rot and decay as far as I'm concerned / the woman in the subway earlier looked at me as if she understood everything only I **78** don't understand anything anymore / I'm constantly asking myself how everyday will be / starting now and if you even thought about how far I'd have to fly with these rotting roses **80** and then not be able to present them to you / I'll party all night **82** like the kids do and have a good time / everyone smiles here / I'll smile all night long too / it'll be easy I swear / no one will **84** notice that something's missing / I'll stay up all night and I especially **86** won't notice that something's missing / missing / and I'll stop asking these pointless questions **88** I'll go to the dogs yet in this town / feels like there's three or four of ,em / towns I mean and people here: all like fish in water only I can't stop thinking about the kite we **90** flew last fall and how we wondered what the world looked like through its eyes high up there in the sky / dark and angular you said and I thought you weren't being very romantic / let's fly away anywhere you cried / so why'd you have to come **92** here of all places without me where everyone keeps on running and smiling and running / almost everyone / I'm the only one who doesn't know how to do it anymore and I think that soon / soon I think / I'll just stop in the middle of this tangle of dead ends and one way streets **94** if the world won't then at least I will / I'll stop here and breathe in emptiness / sorry about the thing with the roses / I could've put ,em on the ground right here in the middle of this foreign city silence **96** the puddles are water hose children no sign of rain anywhere / the cemetery's gotta be around here somewhere the one you chose for your time of stopping / it'll be swarming with strangers half the city'll be there and me in the heart of it and the roses in the hotel and you in the thundering earth which **98** rattles and booms all sun burnt and in hope of water for tomorrow / everyday

THANKS TO

The entire Actar team *for believing in us, giving us hope, and having faith in our work.* Special thanks to: *Anna, Ramon, Dolors, Rein – we love you! Thank you for believing in us!* **All the authors** *for giving this project depth:* László Csiba, Radek Knapp, Sudabeh Mohafez, José F.A. Oliver, Selim Özdogan, Ilija Marinow Trojanow. **All the font-designers** who contributed: *Peter Brugger, Stefan Claudius, Escobas, René Verkaart, Sirkka Hammer, Martina Hartmann, Sandra Hofacker, Paul Hoppe, David Hubner, Boris Kahl, Matthias Kantereit, Ingo Krepinsky, Heinrich Lischka, Michel M., Thomas Mettendorf, Christoph Rankers, Dan Reynolds, Henry Roussier, Christoph Seiler.* **All the MAGMA team** *Sandra Augstein, Daniela Stulic, Sabine Reckwell, Susanne Schwarz, Monika Frondorf, Thomas Mettendorf, Christoph Seiler, Boris Kahl, Flo Gaertner: for helping us get this project up and running.* **Andreas "AL" Lehnert,** www.lunatic-media.de: *for being mister music, always pushing the buttons.* **Andreas Hirsch,** Hirschreisen. **Anna Tetas,** Actar: *you've done a great job!* **Benni Schmidt-Hansberg** *for linking us up with Peter in MXC, you rule, man!* **Boris Kahl,** Magma *for nice font designs and lots of love and patience with Lars and Uli.* **CHR15** *for being strict, direct and severe.* **Corinne and Tom Barbereau** *love for letting us go. Tom, this book shows your future.* **Dee / munit.org** *for all sound specialist expertise.* **Diki Hertel** *for helping us in L.A.* **Diya Ajit** *for all the lovely e-mails and great design, next time we really must meet!* **Dr. Latex** *(p. 341): for opening up your home and office to us and showing us your work.* **Escobas** *(p. 342): for being a wrestling fan, party man, font designer.* **Fakir/Javo** *(p. 341) you rock! Great work, we love you and your friends! Thanx for linking us up to Complot!* **Frank W. Albers,** Robert Bosch Stiftung *for linking us up with the authors.* **Gunilla Zedigh** *for all fine translation work.* **Jakob** *(p. 370),* Cyclos Mesanjeros *Crazy Dansk Torero.* **John Wu** *(p. 360):* VJ, designer, master of speed, Hong Kong will see us again because of you! **Jörg Lesser,** Reisebüro Lesser *Mister 1000 volt-flight-checker. Thanks for organizing our trip!* **Jürgen Siebert,** Fontshop *for the wonderful portrait of your 10 year old daughter Marie Fischer, originaly digitalised by Kai Vermehr (2004, eBoy) – p. 162.* **Katrin Ernst, Gloria Ernst** *(p. 188) wife, mother, beloved, for letting us go.* **Kristina Stifter** *for having faith in us, trusting in us for so many years. Thank you so much!* **Leica**: *support (Leica CM).* **Lutz Frischmann** *Freelens.* **Maria Palatini** *for proofreading the English.* **Marika Jox** *sun, light and fruit tea.* **Martin Wrede** *our man in Berlin.* **Martina Hartmann** *for your illustration p. 160. Stay tuned!* **Martina Weber** *for all your thoughts and constructive criticism.* **Matthias von der Ahe** *photo mac power!* **Michael Schmidt,** Starshot *for linking us up with Eastpak.* **Natalie Ouard,** Emirate Airlines *(p. 164) for opening up your home to us in Dubai. We loved your place! Great pool!* **Nobuhiro Sonoda** *next time you'll be in Tokyo, we hope!* **Peter Kienzle** *for good connections & English.* **Peter Aagaard** *(p. 370),* Cyclos Mesanjeros *for helping us in Mexico City.* **PTV AG** *for supporting this project.* **Ralf Stockhoff** *pope of photobacks!* **Ramon Prat,** Actar *we love your books!* **Recep and Holger** *driving staff & airport-service. Fixie Inc rocks!* **Renko Heuer** *who knows everybody!* **Rieke Harmsen,** EPV *for finding the authors for us, and having great ideas.* **Rüdiger John** *for writing theory, asking strange questions and making us argue.* **Sabine Weinbrecht, Lara & Lazlo Weiß** *wife, daughter and son:* look at this great book! **Sandra Looke** *for giving me a small Leica.* **Sigrid Frank-Eßlinger** *for reading, providing food for thought, lots of help and a fresh pair of eyes.* **Sigrid Ingenohl** *for linking us up with Andreas Hirsch. Yes, the world is out there!* **Stefan G. Bucher,** *(p. 353)* 344design.com *for showing us the Pasadena Art College. We love your design (p. 175).* **Tanja,** EastPak *for providing us perfect Eastpak travel bags.* **Taro Hirano** *(p. 370) for showing us his small studio in Japan (f*** hard to find you!).* **Thomas Mettendorf,** Magma *for the wonderful font Copy and many good ideas.* **Tinka Heeckt** *(p. 70, 359) crazy power girl in Hong Kong. You and your friends are great (p. 371)!* **Top Ev. Berlin**: *Thank you!* **Will Matthews** *Toys and Towers.*

Published by Actar

Editors & Book Designers Christian Ernst, Lars Harmsen, André Rösler, Ulrich Weiss, www.bastard-project.com

Authors László Csiba, Ruediger John, Radek Knapp, Sudabeh Mohafez, José F.A. Oliver, Selim Özdogan, Ilija Marinow Trojanow

Translation Gunilla Zedigh

Volume Editor Sigrid Frank-Eßlinger

Music Andreas Lehnert

Printing Ingoprint SL

Distribution

Actar D

Roca i Batlle 2

E-08023 Barcelona

Tel: +34 93 417 49 93

Fax: +34 93 418 67 07

office@actar-d.com

ISBN 84-96540-15-4

DL B-3699-06

Special thanks to the Robert Bosch Stiftung Stuttgart for their generous
support and helpful connections to the authors.